THE NEW TRIAL

Duke University Press   Durham and London 2001

PETER WEISS

Translated, with an introduction, by James Rolleston and Kai Evers

© 2001 Duke University Press
All rights reserved
Printed in the United States of America
on acid-free paper ∞
Typeset in Quadraat by Tseng Information Systems, Inc.
Caution: The play printed in this volume is designed
for the reading public only. All dramatic, motion picture,
radio, television, and all other rights in the play are fully
protected by all signatories to the Universal Copyright
Convention as well as the Berne Convention, and no public
or private performances—professional or amateur—may
be given without written permission of the copyright
owners. All inquiries about performance rights should be
addressed to the Agent for the play: Ms. Toby Cole, 2951
Derby Street, Berkeley, California 94705.
Originally published as *Der Neue Prozess,*
© Suhrkamp Verlag, Frankfurt am Main, 1984
Library of Congress Cataloging-in-Publication Data appear
on the last printed page of this book.

CONTENTS

PREFACE

The New Trial, Peter Weiss's last play, was produced in English for the first time at Duke University in November 1998. The occasion was a conference organized to survey and reassess the late work of Weiss, who died in 1982, particularly his great novel *The Aesthetics of Resistance*. The organizers of the conference were Julia Hell, Fredric Jameson, and James Rolleston, and it was attended by the author's widow, Gunilla Palmstierna-Weiss, who contributed wonderfully to the discussions. We are grateful to her and to the principal sponsors of the conference—the Swedish Institute, the German Academic Exchange, and the Max Kade Foundation—for initiating the process that has made possible the present publication.

A special feature of the conference was that it gave expression to many of Weiss's creative dimensions: in addition to the Duke Players' production of *The New Trial*, there was an exhibition of his artwork and a showing of rare short films that he made in the 1950s. We have sought to convey something of that variety in this publication: the translation is designed, as far as possible, to be a truly theatrical text and was modified in the course of rehearsals to enhance its spoken quality. We also present discussions and stage images from the original 1982 production at the Dramaten Theater, Stockholm, directed by Peter Weiss, as well as reflections by Jody McAuliffe, the director of the Duke production. Our hope is to stimulate a more intense and nuanced reception of Peter Weiss than exists presently in this country.

Finally, we want to express our appreciation of our editorial assistants, Norma Dockery and Lou Ellen Andrews, who resolutely kept track of this constantly evolving text.

INTRODUCTION
The Theater of Peter Weiss

Almost twenty years after his death in 1982, Peter Weiss is today considered one of the most important writers of German postwar literature. Always an outsider, as often denounced as celebrated during his lifetime by literary critics, politicians, and fellow writers, Weiss has emerged as one of the few writers whose work survived the postunification reevaluation of literature in Germany. Curiously enough, amid the widespread criticism directed by mostly conservative critics at mainstream writers such as Heinrich Böll, Christa Wolf, and Günter Grass, Weiss has been named again and again as the author of some of the finest literary achievements in postwar German literature. Given these attacks against formerly canonical works and writers, it has become fashionable to claim the term "outsider" for a writer. In Weiss's case, however, that term is accurate.

Geographically, politically, or in the context of literary debates, Peter Weiss always insisted, even at the height of his fame, on his position at the margin of Germany's cultural and political life. A Jew according to the racial laws of the Third Reich, he and his parents survived in Swedish exile. Weiss became a Swedish citizen in 1946 and, except for visits, never lived in Germany again. In the late 1940s, Weiss published his first literary texts, but in Swedish, not German. His career as a German writer did not begin until 1960, when, at the age of forty-four and after four books of prose in Swedish, he published *The Shadow of the Body of the Coachman*. This experimental text immediately established Weiss as one of the most innovative writers in German, and its surrealist influence revived a literary tradition that had almost disappeared from postwar German literature. In the 1960s, when Weiss's documentary theater made him Germany's preeminent playwright, he thwarted attempts to make him Germany's literary representative by embracing socialism, by his anti–Vietnam War activities, and especially by reminding West Germany of its Nazi past in his play *The Investigation*.

Between 1972 and 1980, Weiss worked on his magnum opus, *The Aesthetics of Resistance*, a wide-ranging novel about the antifascist resistance movements in Europe from the late 1930s to 1947 that describes the search for the fusion of radical art and politics, a search that becomes—in the form of Weiss's novel—its own realization. Harsh criticism in both Germanys initially "welcomed" each of the three volumes of his monumental novel. In his notebooks, Weiss summed up the initial reactions: "In one Germany the book is published and publicly condemned, in the other Germany it is forbidden and secretly praised." Today, the formerly scandalous novel has not only become a cult book of the Left but has also been recognized as one of the great modernist achievements of postwar Germany. Although *The Aesthetics of Resistance* is now frequently compared to the masterworks of Joyce, Musil, and Proust, during his own lifetime Weiss was primarily known not as a novelist but rather as one of the greatest playwrights of his generation, named in the same breath with Brecht and Beckett.

With *Marat/Sade* (1964), Peter Weiss became overnight a national and international star in the theater world. Set in a mental asylum in postrevolutionary France, the highly theatrical clash between the anarchist revolutionary Marat and the extreme individualist de Sade shattered the boundaries of postwar Germany's theater. Weiss, whose works not only fused Artaud's theater of cruelty with Brecht's epic theater but also incorporated pantomime, bawdy ballads, and elements of classical tragedy, was celebrated as Germany's first great playwright since Brecht. The unresolved confrontation between Marat and de Sade, between the political activist and the libertarian, polarized its audiences, opening up a space for identification and repulsion that, in the midst of the Cold War, proved successful with both West Germans (who favored de Sade) and East Germans (who favored Marat).

The play's triumph immediately transcended national borders. Peter Brook's staging of the play with the Royal Shakespeare Company in

London and on Broadway as well as his film version secured its worldwide fame. Susan Sontag praised *Marat/Sade* as one of the truly great theater experiences of a lifetime. Performed on all five continents and translated into more than fifteen languages, the play continues to be a bestseller, having sold almost half a million copies in Germany alone. At the age of forty-eight, having been a largely unknown painter, filmmaker, film theorist, and writer of experimental prose, Peter Weiss was suddenly celebrated as Germany's preeminent playwright. Older than Wolfgang Borchert and Böll, Weiss established himself as a writer at the same time as much younger authors such as Johnson, Grass, and Walser, whereby his experimental prose influenced a still younger generation, ranging from Ror Wolf to Hubert Fichte.

In 1965, the year after *Marat/Sade*, Weiss confirmed his newly won status as Germany's leading dramatist with his next play. *The Investigation*, a recasting of the Auschwitz trial in Frankfurt, remains one of the most successful and controversial works of literature on the Nazi genocide. The play established Weiss as the German author who did the most for Germany's dawning confrontation with its Nazi past. Unlike Rolf Hochhuth in *The Deputy*, Weiss avoids any direct representation of Auschwitz. As Lawrence Langer notes, *The Investigation* "gradually narrows the space separating the imagination from the camp." Eschewing the brilliant fireworks of *Marat/Sade*, with its two infamous historical title characters at its center, the austere *Investigation* uses a completely different aesthetics. Almost static, without any dramatic stage action, and with an anonymous dramatis personae, the play relies entirely on words—the testimonies in court—to convey the horror and the logic of the camp.

The play's importance and timeliness were recognized immediately, even before its first staging. On 19 October 1965, *The Investigation* premiered simultaneously in fifteen theaters in East and West Germany. Helene Weigel, Brecht's widow, directed a scenic reading for the East German Academy of Arts. Like *Marat/Sade*, it became an instant international success, attracting such leading directors as Ingmar Bergman and, again, Peter Brook. In Europe as well as in the United States, adaptations for television brought *The Investigation* to a large audience. It became the most powerful example of documentary theater in Germany. Weiss used the court testimonies almost verbatim, often only slightly rhythmicizing the language. During the controversy over the Holocaust monument, Jürgen Habermas remembered *The Investigation* as a central occasion in Germany's postwar construction of a collective identity that refuses to repress its murderous past.

Between 1964 and 1975, Weiss wrote nine major plays, provoking several political and aesthetic controversies in both Germanys. Shortly before the premiere of *The Investigation*, Weiss published in *Dagens Nyheter* and in *Neues Deutschland* his "Ten Working Points of an Author in the Divided World," which documents his conversion to socialism. Beginning with *The Investigation*, his emphatic siding with socialism, the German Democratic Republic (GDR), and revolutionary movements in developing countries often invited polemical rejections of his literary works in West Germany. Conservative as well as liberal critics, while still acknowledging Weiss as one of the few important German writers of his generation, blamed his turn to socialist politics and documentary theater for a supposed wilting of his aesthetic powers. Plays like the *Discourse on the Progress of the Prolonged War of Liberation in Viet Nam* and *Song of the Lusitanian Bogey* disappeared almost immediately, after the initial scandal, from Western stages. West Germany's most important literary prize, the Georg Büchner Prize, was awarded to Weiss only after his death in 1982. In 1966, the GDR awarded him the prestigious Heinrich Mann Prize, but it would soon find out that the famous author could be a thorn in its ideological flesh. While always aiming to remain a supporter of the socialist state, Weiss criticized the GDR for the expulsion of Wolf Biermann and provoked it with *Trotsky in Exile* as much as the *Viet Nam Discourse* provoked the West. Official admonition abounded, and his open letters and essays found virtually no outlets inside the GDR. East Germans were not allowed to read *The Aesthetics of Resistance* until eight years after the publication of the first volume in the West.

With *The New Trial* (1982), Weiss not only returned his attention to the stage, he also returned to Kafka's novel *The Trial*. Given Weiss's own position at the margin of German literature, it might not come as a surprise that he had a lifelong interest in Kafka, another writer of Jewish origin with an interest in socialist ideas, who also wrote German in a basically non-German environment, and who also became a towering influence in German literature only after his death. *The New Trial*, a free adaptation of Kafka's novel finished only few months before Weiss's death, marked a new start for him. Although he had been a filmmaker in the 1940s and 1950s in Sweden, Weiss directed his own play for the first time, in collaboration with his wife, Gunilla Palmstierna-Weiss. After the long and exhausting work on his novel, he planned to concentrate again on work for the stage. His plans for future theatrical works were energized by his ability to write the play in just four months, a pace made possible by his long familiarity with the novel and with Kafka's world. He had read the novel as early as 1940 and wrote his first adaptations of *The Trial* in the early 1970s. Weiss's dramatizations of Kafka's *The Trial* thus frame his work on *The Aesthetics of Resistance*.

In 1974, Weiss interrupted his work on the first volume of *The Aesthetics of Resistance* to follow Ingmar Bergman's suggestion that he adapt Kafka's novel for Bergman's theater, the Dramaten. Staying as close as possible to the original text, Weiss intended to disappear as an author behind Kafka's work. He saw his role as that of one who "only searches for theatrical means that can do justice to the content of the book." In a short preface to the play, he stated, "It seemed absurd to me to undertake translations that would transpose the material into a style that would reflect either the excesses of my own invention or the need to adapt to various 'contemporary' issues."

Nevertheless, the play is imbued with Weiss's hope for political revolution. Emphasizing K's social and political existence, Weiss blames Josef K's demise on his failure to understand his position in a class society and to act against it accordingly. Expecting a "bold experiment" and a "personal interpretation," Bergman was disappointed by such sterile faithfulness to both Kafka and dogmatic socialism, and he rejected Weiss's *Trial* for the Dramaten. At least in the West, this simplified reading of Kafka quickly disappeared, as Weiss himself noted, into the trash bin of modern theater. The play's failure reinforced Weiss's own doubts about the possibility of putting Kafka's novel on stage. He also fulfilled Theodor Adorno's prediction in his *Notes on Kafka* that any attempt at dramatizing Kafka's novels is not only doomed to failure but, even worse, would mock some of the greatest artworks of the twentieth century.

But *The New Trial*, Weiss's second attempt to bring Kafka's novel to the stage, met with positive critical response and is now considered to be a culmination of Weiss's quest for a theatrical aesthetics. Using some events and many of the characters from the novel as his starting point, Weiss then combined elements characteristic of his early work, from surrealism to the literature of the grotesque, with his later interest in a literature of engagement to rethink the relationship between aesthetics and resistance in the age of the global market. Weiss considered *The New Trial* his most spontaneous and personal play, one in which he not only expressed his doubts about his own aesthetics and politics, but also addressed Adorno's question as to whether the subject could still have any hope for freedom in the age of late capitalism, and whether any potential for resistance to capitalism remains in aesthetics. *The New Trial*, full of Weiss's own inventions and experiences, comes much closer to what Bergman might have hoped for.

Weiss's rewriting of Kafka to give voice to his own struggles follows the logic of his oeuvre; the process of identifying with and distancing himself from Kafka is a structuring force of Weiss's works throughout his literary career. Kafka's importance for Weiss reaches far beyond his attempts to dramatize *The Trial*. As early as the early 1940s, the Kafka novel had become, according to Weiss, his "central reading experience." Throughout his life, Kafka would remain a point of reference for Weiss. More precisely, Kafka represented for Weiss one of two extreme poles that structure his whole work.

In his first reading of *The Trial*, Weiss identified completely with Kafka. The similarity of their backgrounds—the estrangement from family, culture, and language—has often been noted. As in Kafka, the experience of writing German in a non-German environment left indelible traces in Weiss's relationship to language, to literature, and to Germany. Weiss never identified himself as a German. After his exile from Germany and his attempts to write in Swedish, German became, as he once claimed, not much more than a "tool among other tools."

Reading and identifying with Kafka in 1940 initiated a process of self-reflection for Weiss that made him aware of his own isolation. He found in Kafka his own tendency to succumb to authority. As Weiss wrote, Kafka and Josef K "held me tightly in the sweet erotics of humiliation." In his 1962 autobiographical novel *Vanishing Point*, Weiss describes his extensive readings, which included many of the great modernist achievements of German literature, from Rilke, Musil, and Canetti to Döblin, Jahnn, and Thomas Mann. Kafka's novels *The Castle* and *The Trial*, however, provoked a far more existential reaction in the young Weiss.

> In all the books that revealed their worlds to me so that I might recognize myself in them, there remained always possibilities of retreat into a mysticism, or a notion of beauty, or an idyll, or an illusion of love. In all the books were limitations of risk and escape clauses that ceased to be available in Kafka's report. . . . By reading *The Trial*, I thus became fully alert to the trial that kept me myself prisoner.

The period of identification with Kafka, however, was followed by an identification of Kafka with the world that oppressed and stifled Weiss. Attraction and identification provoked repulsion. For Weiss, Kafka, Josef K, and the world of the novels became a closed totality, a crypt, from which he needed to escape. The recognition of being part of Kafka's world moved Weiss, as he said in an interview, toward revolt, toward a breaking down of the walls of this "completely twisted, guilt ridden, cursed, and damned world of Philistines": a revolt not only against the world Kafka describes, but also against Kafka himself.

Unlike Elias Canetti, who considered Kafka not only the greatest expert on power but also one who offered strategies to escape from it, Weiss read Kafka not merely as a victim of power, but as a victim who succumbs to and affirms his own death sentence.

> Basically, Kafka glorified the dominant authority, he humiliated himself constantly before it, he was fascinated by it; as soon as he found himself beginning to see through it, he sank immediately to the ground to ask its forgiveness. K held me tightly in the sweet erotics of humiliation. All the longing for death inside myself bound itself tightly to his descriptions of total annihilation. For a long time I lived as a suicide, surrounded by images of sickness until they slowly burned themselves out; then I could penetrate to their sources, to their roots.

To overcome his own longings for humiliation and self-destruction, longings that fueled the most powerful images of his early works, Weiss had to distance himself from Kafka. Only through distance was it possible for him to analyze the social and political roots of such desires. In an interview at the time of the premiere of *The Investigation* in 1966, Weiss said that he could write the play only because he kept himself removed from Kafka.

> Ten years ago I could not have written this play because I did not have the openness towards the world which I have today. I could have written it only as being part of Kafka's world, as a subjective nightmare. I would have identified myself with the prisoners. Today I can assume an objective point of view.

Although Weiss's claim to an objective point of view, one that overcomes Kafka's subjectivism, sounds a bit like Lukács's condemnation of Kafka, and although he repeatedly claimed to have left Kafka behind, Weiss always returned to Kafka. Despite his own assertion, Kafka's world kept haunting Weiss; it remained up to the end an integral part of Weiss's oeuvre.

Weiss needed again and again to repeat his liberation from Kafka as a precondition for his own writing. Indeed, one finds an indication of Kafka's crucial significance for Weiss in his contradictory statements about the end of his Kafka phase. The comment cited above about *The Investigation* would put the end of this phase in the mid-1950s at the earliest. In 1964, Weiss told an interviewer that the end of his identification with Kafka coincided more or less with the end of World War II. "In 1940, I began to read Kafka seriously, and when the war was over, my Kafka phase was already largely over, too. Then came Henry Miller." Rather than searching for the "accurate" date of the end of Weiss's Kafka phase, one could reach a clearer understanding of the importance of Kafka for Weiss by following through on his reference to Henry Miller. His rather curious sequence of influence from Kafka to Miller—restated in *Fluchtpunkt*—leads to an unpublished text in which Weiss best characterized Kafka's importance for his own writing. In "Kafka's and Miller's America," drafted during his work on *Fluchtpunkt*, Weiss says: "In Miller and Kafka, I found two poles of my own self. In the one pole was focused the tiredness, the morbid, everything in me that longed to drown, the over-civilized, the satiated quality of the European; in the other pole was concentrated the counter force of wildness, excess, the unfettered, the carnal." Miller would soon lose his function as a counterforce to Kafka. In Weiss's *Aesthetics of Resistance*, Kafka's *Castle* finds its place among the artworks discussed, but nothing resembling its counterforce of excess and sexual transgression. In an interview in 1979, Weiss explained the absence with reference to Miller's individualistic and subjective form of liberation: Miller's excesses seemed useless for an alliance of art and socialism against fascism. Rather than posing an alternative to Kafka's world, Miller seemed to Weiss to be just a part of it.

The temptation to succumb to Kafka's world, to give up, to let go of life, to be fascinated with tortured and dying bodies (besides *The Trial*, Weiss was especially attracted by Kafka's stories *The Judgment* and *In the Penal Colony*) remained a permanent feature of Weiss's experience. The various characters in *The Aesthetics of Resistance* often become for the reader individuals—with an almost bodily presence—only in the moment of death, in Weiss's spare-no-detail descriptions of their agonies. Although Weiss lost interest in Miller's world of individual excess and untrammeled sexuality, one of the qualities ascribed to Miller did survive as a counterforce to Kafka. In a 1964 interview, Weiss praised Miller for his drastic realism and especially his "complete control in describing himself in any situation, his not being afraid of anything or anybody."

The fearless observing eye and the ability to describe everything (not only himself, as Miller did), including purgatory, hell, and paradise, is the central attraction of the only other author whose influence on Weiss equals and contains Kafka's: Dante, the other extreme pole structuring Weiss's works. With Dante, Weiss could walk through Auschwitz and write *The Investigation*.* This play consists of eleven songs, each

---

*Weiss's initial idea for *The Investigation* had Dante and Giotto walking through the camp. The play, originally planned under the title *Paradiso*, was supposed to be part of his three-part project for a contemporary *divina commedia*. Arno Schmidt drew the connection between Dante's *Divina Commedia* and concentration camps as early as the late 1940s. But just as Weiss could find in Kafka nothing but a manual for submission,

of them divided into three parts. This equals thirty-three, the same number of cantos that Dante wrote for his *Paradiso*, which was also Weiss's first title for his play. While for Weiss, Kafka stands for fascination with victimization, torture, and death, he needed Dante to find a form to describe the seemingly ungraspable horror of this century. Referring to his attendance at the Auschwitz trial, Weiss writes in his *Exercise for a Drama in Three Parts on the "Divina Commedia"*:

> I already lost the possibility to speak when I tried to capture the impressions of this tribunal and when I attempted to imagine the events that provided the basis for these proceedings. My thoughts failed me when I thought of the wide-ranging implications of what was alluded to here. Despite countless attacks of despondency and exhaustion, Dante succeeded in finding words for a material that belonged to everybody yet seemed incomprehensible, and what so far had evaded language could now be heard.

With Dante, Weiss overcomes an identification with victims that left no way out of the nightmare. Dante offers Weiss a way to grasp events in language that previously seemed outside his artistic reach, events that Weiss associates with Kafka's world but that now, in a new, more distanced, Dantesque form, could not only determine the cause of the nightmare but also offer an alternative to the nightmarish world from which Kafka, at least from Weiss's perspective, was incapable of escaping. The narrator of *The Aesthetics of Resistance* discusses Dante's poem extensively with his friends and, like Weiss himself, finds Dante essential for the project of finding signs and symbols that describe and survive the fascist terror of annihilation.

In his early prose works, which were strongly influenced by Kafka, Weiss described societies whose impermeable walls remain insurmount-

---

Schmidt saw in Dante's *Inferno* not a form for expressing horror and revulsion, but rather a handbook for torturers. Schmidt wrote a fictive letter to Dante—addressing him in Berlin at the Reichssicherheitshauptamt (Department for Planning of Concentration Camps)—that begins: "With the greatest interest I have read your ambitious 'Inferno, Handbook for Designing Concentration Camps' and take the liberty to express my deeply felt gratitude to you: the trim volume belongs on the shelf of every honest thinking man."

able. Attempting to escape from certain death, the protagonist of *From Island to Island* (1944) runs against a monstrous wall time and time again until he dies: "The last thing that I imagined feeling was the shuddering of the wall." Dreams of imprisonment, as in his story "The Stranger" (1948), and the inability to escape even if the prison's doors should open often terrorize Weiss's characters: "The prison was open. That was the terrible thing. One could have gone outside and yet one stayed put." In his first play, *The Tower* (1948), Weiss wrote of an attempted escape from Kafka's world. The protagonist, Pablo, an escape artist in the circus, had fled in despair from the tower's repressive society of his childhood, only to realize that outside its walls he remained bound by it. He returns to repeat his liberation. Torn between nightmarish reality and the reality of a nightmare, the end of the play remains unresolved: did Pablo hang himself in his final escape, or did he destroy the world of the tower?

In the 1960s, then, Weiss's turn against Kafka's world becomes far more explicit and determined. His carnivalesque play *How Mr. Mockinpott Is Cured of His Sufferings* (1963/1968), the title character of which finds himself at the beginning imprisoned for no apparent reason, has been read as a parody of Kafka's *Trial*. Filled with scenes of slapstick, Mockinpott's itinerary of suffering ends in a revolt against God, an old cigar-smoking man who leaves, broken, while Mockinpott dances off the stage.

Weiss's next phase, his turn to documentary theater, leaves parody behind. It represents a direct attack on Kafka's world. Weiss's explicit goal was to defeat a position that he associated very strongly with Kafka: instead of mere descriptions of despair and hopelessness, the documentary theater should participate in the analysis of its causes and provide strategies for their overcoming.

Documentary theater thus revolts against a drama that turns its own despair and anger into its main theme and that clings to the concept of a hopeless and absurd world. Documentary theater stands for the alternative that reality, however impenetrable it may appear to be, can be explained in each and every detail. It would be misleading to suggest that Weiss abandoned earlier literary influences—surrealism, the decidedly modern aesthetics of shock, the fascination with the motif of torture—for an entirely rationalized documentation and explanation of the terror of history that puts itself in the service of a future socialism. Instead, his fascination with the *Divina Commedia* on the aesthetic level and his embrace of socialism on the political level provided Weiss with a framework that allowed for an uncompromising confrontation with death and destruction, be it the terrifying account of phenol injections in Auschwitz or the agonizing images of the execution of resistance fighters at the end of *The Aesthetics of Resistance*. Dante and socialism function not as replacements for Kafka's world but as means to encounter it without falling silent. For Weiss as well as for the protagonists of *The Aesthetics of Resistance*, Dante offers a model of an aesthetics that overcomes the silencing threat of annihilation, a method "in which the terror of annihilation overcame itself by leaving signs behind that survive its own duration." All of Weiss's literary works, culminating in *The Aesthetics of Resistance*, describe the search for a contemporary aesthetics that might preserve and spread a potential of resistance, despite the persistent threat of complete destruction and the danger of a conformity to the market that leaves no space for any political or aesthetic alterity.

The New Trial provides the stage for Weiss's most personal and self-critical exploration of the problem of whether or not aesthetics remains capable of furthering resistance. Weiss returns to Kafka together with Dante. Among the many artworks that the stage directions list for K's apartment is Dante's bust. Like *The Investigation*, *The New Trial* follows Dante's example in being divided into thirty-three scenes. But *The New Trial* does not represent a simple overcoming of Kafka's world of hopelessness and despair through Dante's powers of description and detachment. The play is critical and doubtful about the possibility of resistance in a social system that draws energy from every impulse that aims at its destruction.

Instead of opening with the arrest of the protagonist, *The New Trial* chronicles K's stellar career in his company. The higher he rises, the more he understands that his arguments for social change are nothing but a public relations ploy behind which the company generates ever further expansion. Besides being the supposed moral consciousness of the international conglomerate, K functions as the company's art expert. In order to acquire paintings for its new representative building, K makes contact with Titorelli. Weiss puts Titorelli's paintings into

a constellation with images by Uccello, Piero della Francesca, Géricault, and Rivera, all of them works that were analyzed in his novel as
promising models for an aesthetics of resistance. Titorelli's paintings
seem to possess the same potential for such an aesthetics. His images
of social injustice, oppression, and suffering challenge the military,
political, and economic leaders who come to celebrate the opening
of the new building. A general sees them as so incendiary, he fears
they might contain actual explosives that could blow up the whole
company. But Weiss does not share this naïveté about the political
potential of aesthetics. The representatives of power begin to appreci-
ate the artworks. They hang the paintings on the walls of their offices
as signs of their tolerance, their ability to feel the pain of those who
are suffering under their regime. Titorelli's paintings become deco-
rative pieces in corporate headquarters, a "humane" front that covers
up the aggressive expansion of the military and business operations.
The end of the play seems to leave no room for hope: critical political movements decay into parties defending the status quo, and the
easily suppressed revolt in the last scene of the play expresses nothing
but despair.

The impression that Weiss returned in his last play to Kafka's world, a
world without exit, is, however, only half of the truth. Realizing the
limitations of an aesthetics of resistance, K comes close to dismiss-
ing art altogether. Leni, probably the most politically astute character
in the play, defends art's potential against K's objections by repeating
the insight that the protagonists of *The Aesthetics of Resistance* arrived
at in their encounter with Dante's *Divina Commedia*: "It's no contradiction to make a sign pointing to the suffering that would tear you
apart. It's no contradiction to make eternal what will disappear in an
instant."

Art can leave behind a sign that survives the suffering, the terror of annihilation. That the same artworks might also function as decorations
for corporate culture only attests to their ability to survive. Art itself
cannot resist anything, yet it contains messages that can be decoded
and used in the future, just like the paintings and novels analyzed in
The Aesthetics of Resistance. They too were owned, preserved, and appro-
priated by the ruling elite—decorations whose subversive messages
have to be deciphered again and again. And aesthetics has another,

more immediate function in the play. Titorelli never works alone on his paintings; they are collaborative works. Their subjects, from truck drivers to generals, become participants in their making. In the traces these people leave on his paintings, Titorelli finds the power of his artwork. Weiss, describing the staging of *The New Trial*, never tired of emphasizing that his production was also a collaborative effort, an endeavor that engaged author, actors, stage designer, and everybody else involved. According to Weiss's *The New Trial*, only in such a participatory effort of decoding can the potential of any artwork be understood and made effective.

CHRONOLOGY

1916 Born on 8 November in Nowawes, near Berlin, son of Eugen Weiss, owner of a textile factory, and Frieda Weiss, former actress in Max Reinhardt's theater company.

1934 Immigrates with his parents to Chislehurst, England.

1935 First exhibition of his paintings in London. The family moves to Warnsdorf, Czechoslovakia.

1936 Beginning of a correspondence with Hermann Hesse, who praises his drawings. Weiss meets Hesse twice in Montagnola, Switzerland. In October begins to study painting at the Academy of Arts in Prague. Reads the works of Franz Kafka for the first time.

1937 Occupation of northern Bohemia (the Sudetenland). Because of his Jewish origin, Eugen Weiss has to leave Warnsdorff immediately; Peter Weiss remains at first in Switzerland, illustrating two of Hesse's novellas.

1938 The family reunites in Alingsås, Sweden. Peter Weiss works there in his father's new textile factory.

1939 Peter Weiss moves to Stockholm, which will remain his main residence until his death. Studies the works of Kafka extensively.

1940 Exhibition of his paintings in Stockholm.

1941 Works as a lumberjack, textile worker, and farmhand. Continues to work in his father's factory. Attempts to escape his dependence on his father fail repeatedly.

1942 Makes contact with the Fyrtiotalisterna, a group of Swedish writers. Marries Helga Henschen, a Swedish painter; they divorce shortly afterward.

1943   Journey to Paris; influenced by surrealism and experimental film. Reads Henry Miller's *Tropic of Cancer*.

1945   Publishes his first book in Swedish, *From Island to Island* [Från ö till ö]. Travels to France and Germany as a correspondent for the Swedish newspaper *Tidningen*.

1946   His second book, *The Vanquished* [De besegrade], partly based on his articles on Germany, is published in Stockholm. Becomes a Swedish citizen on his thirtieth birthday.

1947   Premiere of his first play, *The Tower* [Der Turm], at the Studie-Scenen, Stockholm, 18 September.

1952–60 Concentrates on his work as a filmmaker and film critic. Produces a number of experimental short films and documentaries as well as two full-length movies. In 1956, he publishes his study *Avant-Garde Film*, which traces the history of film from Georges Méliès to Ingmar Bergman and himself.

1960   Suhrkamp publishes *The Shadow of the Body of the Coachman* [Der Schatten des Körpers des Kutschers]. With this story, written in 1952, Weiss's career as a writer in Germany and in German begins.

1961–62 Publication of his autobiographical story "Leavetaking" ["Abschied von den Eltern"] and his autobiographical novel *Vanishing Point* [Fluchtpunkt]. In 1962, Weiss participates for the first time in a meeting of the Gruppe 47.

1963   Awarded the Charles Veillon Prize for *Vanishing Point*. Premiere of *Night with Guests* [Nacht mit Gästen] at the Schiller Theater, Berlin, 16 November. Marries Gunilla Palmstierna.

1964   Premiere of *The Persecution and Assassination of Jean-Paul Marat as Performed by the Inmates of the Asylum of Charenton under the Direction of the Marquis de Sade (Marat/Sade)* [Die Verfolgung und Ermordung Jean Paul Marats dargestellt durch die Schauspielergruppe des Hospizes zu Charenton unter Anleitung des Herrn de Sade] in the Schiller Theater, Berlin, 29 April. Weiss attends the Frankfurt Auschwitz trial.

1965   Awarded the Lessing Prize from the city of Hamburg. Premiere of *The Investigation* [Die Ermittlung] at the Freie Volksbühne in West Berlin and the German Academy of Arts in East Berlin as well as thirteen other theaters in Germany, 19 October. Ingmar

Bergman stages the play at the Dramaten, Stockholm; stage design by Gunilla Palmstierna-Weiss.

1966   Awarded the Heinrich Mann Prize of the German Academy of Arts (GDR).

1967   Awarded the Carl Albert Anderson Prize, Sweden. Premiere of *Song of the Lusitanian Bogey* [*Gesang vom Lusitanischen Popanz*] at the Scala Teatern, Stockholm, 26 January. Participates in the Vietnam tribunals (Russell tribunals) in Stockholm and Roskilde.

1968   Premiere of *Discourse on the Progress of the Prolonged War of Liberation in Viet Nam and the Events Leading Up to It as Illustration of the Necessity for Armed Resistance against Oppression and on the Attempts of the United States of America to Destroy the Foundations of Revolution* (Viet Nam Discourse) [*Diskurs über die Vorgeschichte und den Verlauf des lang andauernden Befreiungskrieges in Viet Nam als Beispiel für die Notwendigkeit des bewaffneten Kampfes der Unterdrückten gegen ihre Unterdrücker sowie über die Versuche der Vereinigten Staaten von Amerika die Grundlagen der Revolution zu vernichten*] in Frankfurt am Main, 20 March. Premiere of *How Mr. Mockinpott Is Cured of His Sufferings* [*Wie dem Herrn Mockinpott das Leiden ausgetrieben wird*], 16 May.

1969   Premiere of *Trotsky in Exile* [*Trotzki im Exil*] at the Schauspielhaus, Düsseldorf, 20 January. The play's rejection by critics and audiences coincides with the collapse of Weiss's health. He begins writing *Convalescence* [*Rekonvaleszenz*], a diary published posthumously in 1991.

1971   Premiere of *The Assurance* [*Die Versicherung*] at the Städtische Bühnen Essen, 8 April. Premiere of *Hölderlin* at the Württembergisches Staatstheater, Stuttgart, 18 September.

1975   Premiere of *The Trial* [*Der Prozess*], Weiss's adaptation of Kafka's novel, at the Theater der Freien Hansestadt Bremen, 28 June. Publication of the first volume of *The Aesthetics of Resistance* [*Die Ästhetik des Widerstands*].

1976   Comprehensive retrospective of Weiss's paintings and collages at the Södertälje Konsthall, Sweden.

1977   Further exhibitions in Rostock, Munich, Zurich, and Paris.

1978   Awarded the Thomas Dehler Prize. Publication of second volume of *The Aesthetics of Resistance*.

1982   Premiere of *The New Trial* [*Der neue Prozess*], directed by Peter Weiss and Gunilla Palmstierna-Weiss, at the Dramaten, Stockholm, 12 March. Awarded the Prize for Literature of the City of Bremen, the Georg Büchner Prize, and the Prize of the Swedish Theater Critics. Dies on 10 May in Stockholm.

THE NEW TRIAL

Dedicated to Franz Kafka

ACT ONE

Scene 1

[K in bed. Covered with a white sheet. Three men wander around, casting the beams of their flashlights in circles. Furniture and other objects are briefly illuminated. Beside the bed a night table and a chair with clothes lying across it. A closet with a mirror on its door. A chest of drawers. A washstand. A large, oval table with high-backed chairs. Shelves full of books. On the walls, newspaper clippings, slips of paper, and reproductions of pictures by Bosch, Brueghel, Rousseau, and Picasso. In between, illustrations of Don Quixote, of Dante's head, of witch burnings, torture chambers, strange architectural visions. On the floor, statuettes, copies of classic works, for example, Degas's dancer, a Greek torso, a relief by Gauguin. Everywhere stacks of books, piles of newspaper. High on the wall, a crudely glued-on piece of cardboard. In the background, a closed door. Two of the men are in work clothes; one of them has a safety helmet hanging from his belt. They have tools and pockets full of equipment. The third man wears a dark suit. They have placed a box on the floor, open the lid. It is a machine for measuring sounds. A beam focuses on it, then at once sweeps further, to the bed. K still lies motionless, on his side, his legs drawn up. The two workers squat down by the machine, turning levers. The third man goes to the bed, pulls the sheet back.]

K: What is it?

[Two beams are immediately directed at him.]

Franz [one of the workers, with the machine]: Nothing. We've tried to figure out what you mean—but we can't hear a thing.

K: What?

Franz: The disturbance that you're always talking about. The company sent us.

K: Ah . . .

Kaminer [the man in the suit, has taken over the machine and points to its measuring needle]: Only tiny deflections. That's caused by the street-noise . . .

K [sits up. He is naked except for briefs. Turns his head back and forth, listening]: Here, you can hear it here. If you stand completely still, then you'll hear it . . .

[Kaminer holds up the machine, turns it in various directions. Shakes his head.]

K: Such a humming. It must come from the vent.

Willem [beams his flashlight at the piece of cardboard on the wall]: The vent is sealed shut.

K: Because otherwise stuff blows in, with dust . . .

Kaminer: So you shut out the air . . .

K: I can open the window . . .

Kaminer: Then you get dust and noise from outside . . .

K: Better that than the humming—it comes from the motor up there . . .

Willem: We've been on the roof. Checked the motor. It's working fine.

K: It's a very tiny sound. But it keeps me awake. You'd have to come at night . . .

Franz: You are insatiable!

K [raises his head even higher]: Here you can hear it quite plainly . . .

Kaminer [places the machine next to K]: There's nothing! [Points at the box.] There, it's our voices making the needle move—now it's our breathing—now it's some footsteps on the street. [He presses the box against K.] And now it's your heart. There's nothing else. And now it's the door . . .

[The door in the background is opened. Garish light floods in. In the door stand Mrs. Grubach and the Captain. K sinks back down.]

Scene 2

[Mrs. Grubach, the owner of the boardinghouse: an old but vigorous woman; wears an apron; is carrying a tray with breakfast. The Captain, her nephew, wearing the trousers and boots of a uniform and suspenders over an undershirt. The light cuts vividly through the room, passing above the oval table. The rest of the room disappears in darkness. K pulls the sheet over himself. Kaminer stretches out of the shadow above the illuminated table.]

Kaminer: Just as I said. Mrs. Grubach, there simply is no quieter building than yours to be found anywhere. [He switches off the machine.]

Captain: If he were in the country he'd be griping about the birds. Engineer Kaminer, kindly switch off the birds!

Kaminer: He only has to telephone and we come running. I got up two hours early. Went without breakfast—just to help him.

[Mrs. Grubach and the Captain enter. The Captain turns on the light switch by the door. A weak brightness illuminates the parts of the room outside the strong light beam. Willem and Franz are packing up their equipment.]

Mrs. Grubach [setting the table]: Please eat breakfast with us. After all, it's his birthday. We want to celebrate.

Captain: Yes, he's turning thirty. That's when life really begins. Third of July. And with weather like that he's sitting around behind closed curtains.

Mrs. Grubach: Leave him alone. After all, he's always working late at night.

Captain: Working? He's always reading, reading—is that work?

[Willem, Franz, and Kaminer sit down at the table. Mrs. Grubach pours coffee, cuts the cake. The Captain sits down also, spreads out a newspaper.]

Mrs. Grubach [turns to K]: Sir, won't you join us?

[K continues to lie motionless in the bed. Mrs. Grubach sits at the lower end of the table. Coffee is drunk and cake eaten.]

Kaminer [eating noisily]: Take me, for example, I live above the fire station. What a racket there is at night. People sliding down the poles. Crash! Into the trucks. Off they go, sirens blaring. And let me tell you, I've even grown used to that. You get used to everything. If you just want to.

Captain: And I miss life in the barracks. It's not right for an officer to live at home. This place makes me feel like I'm already retired. But perhaps things will get started again soon! [Drums on the table with his fists.]

Franz: You mean there'll be war?

Captain [hits the newspaper]: There's been war everywhere for a long time! Show me the continent where there's no war . . .

Willem: But those aren't real wars!

Franz: Just skirmishes!

Willem: They're at loggerheads about . . . what's it called?. . . . Struggles for liberation . . . liberation from what?

Franz: And then they start beating up on each other right away . . .

Kaminer: Yes, a real war is something else . . .

Captain: Something that demands your whole allegiance!

Kaminer: When I think of the last war!

Mrs. Grubach: Two great wars in my lifetime. I was still a child in the first one. My father got killed in it. And now there'll be another war?

Captain: My dear aunt, that's the way of the world! Look at history. The Greeks, the Persians, the Romans—it's human nature! That's why there must be soldiers. Who defend the country when it's attacked! [*Kaminer pours himself another cup of coffee. He drinks noisily, turns in K's direction.*]

Kaminer: To your health, Mr. Chief Attorney! The directors must think a lot of you. Just think: They send out to you two workers and an engineer . . .

Mrs. Grubach: Mr. Kaminer, he's really very efficient in the company. I heard just recently that he's to be promoted.

Kaminer: Yes, his boss values him. Why exactly? Don't we accomplish just as much? But all we hear is, the chief attorney is indispensable. The chief attorney—without him the whole department would collapse.

Mrs. Grubach: And if he's such a good worker, you should also take care that he feels well. Every day he brings home work from the office. So he shouldn't be disturbed. And the house belongs to the company. After all, he had to leave his old room. We all had to up and leave the beautiful apartment. You know that, Mr. Kaminer. And not everyone finds such a change easy. It's such a big company! I always say: if it says it's for the public welfare, then it should be there for the public . . .

Kaminer [*laughing*]: Public welfare! The truth is the company has to pay for itself . . . [*Wipes his mouth, stands up.*] Good Lord, we'll be late! Let's go, boys, we were supposed to finish things up before working hours! [*Kaminer, Willem, and Franz leave with the box and the tools. Franz puts on the safety helmet.*]

Captain [*hits the newspaper again*]: You're not safe any more in your own city! Muggings in the street! We should bring in the military! [*He jumps up, in the process knocking over the chair. Marches after the others out of the room. Slams the door shut behind him. Mrs. Grubach also gets up. Shakes her head. Goes over to the bed.*]

Scene 3

[*In the weak light the contours of objects in the room are ill defined. The statuettes and stacks of books resemble lumps of clay. A gloomy gray light covers the pictures and slips of paper on the walls. The table, with its jumbled plates and cups, bits of cake, and skewed chairs, looks like a pile of junk. Only the white sheet covering K shines brightly.*]

Mrs. Grubach: You shouldn't let these people intimidate you. Come, let's get dressed now. [*She carefully removes the sheet.*] And as for Miss Bürstner—I wouldn't trust her. I wouldn't run after her so much . . . [*K is about to respond; she puts her hand over his mouth.*] I know, I know. You always want to see the best in people. That's what's so special about you. [*She has taken K's shirt from the chair, slips it over him.*] And if the person turns out differently, you just don't want to believe it.

K: My dear Mrs. Grubach—how shall I say it—I want to understand everything—I explain it to myself—everything should have an explanation, after all—that's it—there really shouldn't be any misunderstandings . . .

[*Mrs. Grubach has taken the stockings from the chair and puts them on him. K slowly slides around and sits on the edge of the bed, lets his trousers too be pulled onto him.*]

Mrs. Grubach: And then everything seems to frustrate you. You've lived so long now in my house. I always used to say to my husband: we could never find a better and friendlier tenant than chief attorney K, he disturbs nobody, does nothing to harm anyone . . . and everything's upside down, he has to break his own back trying to fix everything . . .

K [*as he lets his shirt be tucked into his trousers*]: No, no! It's only sometimes like that—in the morning. Or late evening. Or at night. I think about how this was, how that was. It's easier, much easier during the day. The days just fly by.

Mrs. Grubach [*puts on his shoes, wipes them with her apron*]: Really? But often, when you come home, you immediately start asking questions. Where's the captain? What has the captain been doing? Where's Miss Bürstner? Isn't Miss Bürstner home yet? And my late husband—he liked company but it was too much even for him when you came running right away to his bedside and asked: How are you today? Are you feeling better? Have the pains gotten less? But he knew how things were with him. He'd known since the war. He never recovered from the war. And when he died, you wept as if it had been your own father.

K [*stretches his neck, lets his tie be put on*]: You see . . . dying . . . I think so much about it. Not that I'm afraid of death. No, that's not it. But death, that is the other—and at the same time it's always there. At night I try to imagine what it's like, to be dead. And since your husband had suffered so much, I thought perhaps he could tell me something about it. You see . . . this suffering . . . I deal with it every day in the insurance department . . . The whole point is to find a remedy, to make things easier. Only at night, or rather, at about three in the morning, yes, just before dawn, it all overwhelms me . . . that nothing suffices, that nothing can be solved . . . however perfectly everything is arranged. Yes, Mrs. Grubach, the better my work is going, the less it can achieve. Do you understand?

Mrs. Grubach [*has tied the tie, helps him into his jacket*]: I understand. But don't take it so much to heart. [*She examines him, fetches his hat, puts it on him.*] What a good-looking man you are! How easy everything could be for you. Good work. Good income. And the women, they are crazy about you!

K: The women?

Mrs. Grubach: I keep my eyes open. Here in the boardinghouse ladies come and go. But you've fallen for Miss Bürstner. Give her up, you need someone you can marry. Someone you can make a home with.

K: Mrs. Grubach, to you I can say this, Miss Bürstner has something I just haven't found in anyone else. I don't know what it is. Her eyes perhaps. Or her voice. When I hear her voice, it's like . . . like a shock. In the evening I wait until I hear this voice—through the wall.

Mrs. Grubach: Is that why you're always up at night? Because she always comes so late.

K: Mrs. Grubach . . .

Mrs. Grubach: You must go now. It's high time. People there care nothing that it's your birthday, not in a business like that!

Scene 4

[*Everything that was still recognizable in the room fades out. The pieces of furniture loom disconnectedly out of the semi-darkness. K enters upon a journey full of obstacles. He clambers over the chairs, the table. It is as if he found himself* in a rugged alien landscape. Somewhere on a rise he stops, disappears in some depths, reemerges. Plunges then directly into the daytime world. The office that he enters is perhaps not at all spacious, but suggests affinities to grandiose proportions. Constant movement all around: gesticulating, a babble of voices. City maps of Rome, Paris, London, New York; tables and diagrams. In the foreground two desks. Rabensteiner sits at the left desk. In front of him a mass of papers is spread out. On the desk opposite him letters lie piled up. Here one also sees some objects and shapes similar to those in K's room. Carvings, twigs, shells, stones, pieces of crystal, unusual boxes, photos of cathedrals, temples, other structures. While K sits down at his desk, Rabensteiner assumes an ironic pose, cups his chin in his hand, directs a penetrating gaze at K. K disregards him. Leafs through the letters. Cuts some open.]

K [as if to himself]: And what would it matter if I came late one time? It wouldn't really count as tardiness. I would have already made up the time the evening before. I'm here almost every evening later than everyone else.

Rabensteiner: But you see, that's not how it's calculated. We come into the office and your chair is empty. The mail lies unopened on the table. Messengers come with files from the various departments. Secretaries ask for you. You know how many meetings there are now. And when you stay after closing time, no one notices. You're only here when you're seen. By closing time most things are settled as far as we're concerned. What counts is the morning. That's when things take off. Like when the starter pistol goes off at a race. We really make sure that everyone's there at that moment.

K: That I was late today is due to disagreeable matters for which the company is really responsible. Disturbances that keep me awake all night . . .

Rabensteiner: But people have already been sent out to you several times. The director himself gave the instructions to our construction company. Everything's been done that can be done. Besides, it's only a transitional stage . . .

K: Mr. Rabensteiner, you are mistaken! [Appears absorbed in reading letters.]

Rabensteiner: I'll tell you something. . . . You're always talking about how people's lives should be improved. How we should do more to fight misery. Now misery is really being eliminated, a new world is coming. But as for you—I think you're basically a stick-in-the-mud.

K: There is no transition. Everything is completely fixed, a single system. In my previous apartment everything was just as it is now. I suppose my standpoint has changed somewhat, but my view is the same. [*He returns to reading a letter. Rabensteiner has left his desk and has moved behind K. He reads the letter over K's shoulder along with him.*] Of course every day makes new demands. But the situation is the same. And you, Mr. Rabensteiner, you also remain the same! [*He turns around quickly, thrusts the letter up close to Rabensteiner's face.*]

Rabensteiner [*retreating*]: Ah—it's from the Progressive Party!

K: Do you belong to this party?

Rabensteiner: Me? I don't belong to any party. You know that. The company is enough for me. It's more than a party. When you think how much scope it gives you. And how many people it employs. But you want everything to fit into one category. That's why you look around at parties and attend meetings here and there. You'd really like to be politically active. It seems to me you're always complaining in order to make trouble, to stir things up. No wonder the parties send their publicity to your home. And you—you waste your time with it.

K: Keeping informed is part of my job. The material sent to us by study groups, societies, and parties doesn't concern me alone—that's where the general interest begins. It affects our whole institution. From letters like this I learn what's preoccupying people out in the world, outside our operations.

Rabensteiner: I'm certainly not claiming that you're not knowledgeable in our affairs, I mean inside the insurance company. But what do you know, for example, about the real estate market, about capital transactions, about international involvements? You know about our main affiliates. [*He points to the city maps.*] But what can you say about the relationships between the various managing groups? You think everything is secure and regulated. You only turn to the central office when it's a matter of your trivial personal concerns. And you think you can gain insight by roaming around outside! What arrogance!

K: Mr. Rabensteiner, it's precisely the other way around. It's what's fixed and secure that makes me uncertain. It's solidity and order that make me want to question everything. Not that I'm against order. I want order—but a different kind of order. How can I explain that to you—I want a larger order, an order in which everything makes sense.

Rabensteiner [taps K soothingly on the shoulder]: Yes, yes, just don't get so worked up! Anyway, it was only a joke. Don't you understand a joke anymore? You're alone too much these days. Yes, you always sit around on your own. When I call Mrs. Grubach and ask for the chief attorney—you don't even have your own telephone—she always says he's not available. Why? Is he sick? Does he have visitors? No: he's alone and doesn't want to be disturbed. What does that mean? That's what I meant when I said that you don't live in the same time as the rest of us. . . . But now I'm the one preventing you from working! [He takes a few steps back and leaves.]

Scene 5

[A careworn woman, wearing a head scarf and a blanket for a coat, approaches K from the background. She is followed by two children and some older people, all dressed cheaply and meagerly. The woman approaches K's desk with an obsequious attitude. Her group remains at a distance. K looks up from reading his letter.]

The Woman: This is how it is: in summer it's still OK. But I have to think of fall and winter. How will it be then? We have no heat. Even the gas doesn't work. Now the electricity is out too. When I want to cook, I have to light a fire on the kitchen floor. The furniture was supposed to be sent on to us from the old house: this man promised us . . . I don't know his name . . .

K: Kaminer . . .

The Woman: Kaminer . . . perhaps. When they took us away, they were already smashing in the roof. In the afternoon we ran back—the furniture hadn't come. And then we saw it, lying under the wreckage of the torn-down house.

K: Didn't you apply to the head office? They would of course have been obliged to provide you with new furniture immediately.

The Woman: My father went to the office [she points to one of the old men, who nods in agreement] —and my mother too [the old woman nods eagerly] —I had to stay with the children. And then they came back. They hadn't found anyone. Sure, they'd talked to lots of people, but no one knew anything about it, and then it was closing time and they were told to come back the next day, and the next day they went again and got exactly the same runaround.

**Scene 5: K in his office with the Woman, her group, and Kaminer.
New York map in the background.**

K: And how was the new house?

The Woman: It was even older. Barely a roof over our heads. We lie on the floor. We've collected rags and straw, lie on a few blankets. Hardly anyone else lives in the house. It's set to be torn down also.

K [*opens a desk drawer*]: What's your file number?

The Woman: File number?

K: Don't you have a number, as a tenant?

The Woman [*shakes her head*]: I only have the rental contract. [*Takes a folded document from her cape and hands it to K.*]

K [*opens the tattered document, leafs through the files, pulls out a card and reads it*]: As a company tenant you're automatically entitled to insurance. I'm responsible for insurance contracts. Why did you wait so long?

The Woman: Well, first we thought we were to move out before Christmas. Then at New Year's. And then January passed. The cold! The children had become ill. Mostly we stayed in bed. At that time we still had our beds.

K: And when did you move, then?

The Woman: In February . . . no . . . not till March. My parents were running around to every possible department and it was all I could do to gather wood. [*The people accompanying her draw somewhat closer, bringing the Children with them.*] My husband [*she turns to him as he approaches, nodding*] was looking for work, or else he had to go to the unemployment office to get his money, and my parents just got sent from one official to the next until finally someone who lives upstairs from us tells us we really ought to go to the insurance office.

K [*has read the contract through*]: But the contract expired a long time ago. As far back as New Year's. Have you paid rent this year?

The Woman: Not for the past few months. The man from the office, Mr. . . .

K: Kaminer.

The Woman: He said we didn't have to pay any more. That the company was responding to our need with a special kindness. We would only have to pay again when we moved into the new apartment . . .

K: You would have to renew the rental contract.

The Woman: So it's back to the office? Who should we ask to see there?

K: I will take over this matter. Leave the paper with me . . .

The Woman: No, I'm not letting the contract out of my hand!

K [*hands the Woman the paper*]: It can be done without the contract. You will move into a new apartment as soon as possible.

The Woman: Are you really going to help us?

K: I promise you!

[*Everyone has now moved up close to K. The old people bow several times. The Woman seizes K's hand. One of the Children tries to climb up onto K's chair. He pushes the child away. Presses the button of a machine on the desk.*]

K [*calling into the microphone*]: Mr. Kaminer!

[*Kaminer appears immediately. K is writing something on a piece of paper.*]

K: Mr. Kaminer, there must have been a mistake here. Make sure that this woman is paid the compensation due her. [*Kaminer accepts the paper. K turns to the group.*] Mr. Kaminer will take you to the cashier. Trust me. Be patient for just a while longer.

[*Kaminer pushes the group out roughly. All exit. K arranges his papers. Pushes the objects on the desk back and forth. Contemplates the photographs. Remains sitting in this manner while patches of darkness appear. Finally only pieces of the desk can be seen: K's face and hands. Then everything is dark.*]

Scene 6

[*The room in the boardinghouse, now very bright: everything is clearly outlined, vivid. K and Mrs. Grubach amid the furniture, sculptures, and pictures.*]

K: This morning I hardly said what I felt about her eyes and her voice. I must describe all that to you. The eyes. It's more the shadow under the eyes. There are a few fine lines at the corners of the eyes. When the eyelids are lowered they have a bluish sheen. And the voice—when I hear the sound of that voice I just know that something is there that is capable of changing my whole life. But even that doesn't describe it. The eyes, the voice, those are just signs . . .

Mrs. Grubach: Miss Bürstner was here this afternoon. With a strange man. He asked about you. He was insisting on going into your room. He said it still had something to do with the ventilation. But I didn't let him in. I told him no one is allowed into the chief attorney's room when he's not there.

K: Did he give his name?

Mrs. Grubach: No.

K: What did he look like?

Mrs. Grubach: Well, he was fairly hefty.

K: And Miss Bürstner—did she act familiarly with him?

Mrs. Grubach: Hmm . . . could be. Yes, she put her hand under his arm when she went with him into her room.

K: They went together into her room?

Mrs. Grubach: Yes.

K: How long was he with her? Did they come together, or was he visiting her?

Mrs. Grubach: I don't know. I was in the kitchen. They called for me after a while.

K: Had the man been here before?

Mrs. Grubach: I don't think so. No, I'd never seen him before.

[*Sounds from the boardinghouse interior. A door is opened. Voices. Laughter. Steps approach. The Captain pokes his head in, looks around.*]

Captain: We're taking our summertime walk and this guy's hiding out here. Just as I thought. We're walking by the river, past the castle; the sun is setting, what a sky! And we say—the chief attorney, he's bound to be still sitting in his office. He sees nothing of the sunset. And when he comes home, it's already dark. He's missed the red clouds.

Scene 6: K, Mrs. Grubach. Pictures by Picasso, Henri Rousseau, Brueghel, Bosch.

K: The red clouds . . .

Captain: He saw nothing, because he always walks bent over. All he sees
is the pavement and his worn-out shoes.
[The Captain enters the room, pretends to walk ponderously, his feet pointing
outward.]

Mrs. Grubach: Leave him alone. He's tired.

Captain: Tired! If he's tired, then it's tiredness from too much sitting.
Nothing tires you more than doing nothing but sitting! [He begins a
brisk stride, almost a military march, swings his arms, does an about-face.] If
I had him as a recruit, I'd teach him a thing or two.
[Miss Bürstner appears in the open door. Laughing, she leans against the door
frame. She is wearing a bright summer dress. Her hair is tied up high on her head.
K looks at her, takes a few steps toward her, stops, and stares at her.]

Miss Bürstner [laughing]: Yes, Mr. Chief Attorney, we've been thinking
about you. You're such a recluse. One always wonders: what's he really
thinking? One almost feels guilty looking at you. It's as if you always
knew better. I think you reckon you're something really special, the
way you always keep to yourself.

K: Miss Bürstner . . . I don't want to be all on my own . . .

Miss Bürstner: And then when you say something, it's as if you hadn't been listening at all. You just keep staring straight ahead . . .

K: Miss Bürstner, I'm looking at you . . .

Miss Bürstner: You're looking right through me.

K: Yes, that's quite right! You know, I've been mostly listening to your voice. Whenever I hear your voice, what I'm really hearing is its sound.

Captain: I must repeat: I'm sorry I don't have you out on the parade ground. I'd really like to train you. You'd be good training fodder. [*The Captain goes quickly up to K, grasps his arm, lifts him up, lets him fall, yanks the other arm up, also lifts his leg, swings it to and fro. K just lets everything happen.*]

K: Miss Bürstner—you chose to speak to me! I never wanted to talk to you directly, never dared to. I always wanted you to talk to me first . . .

Mrs. Grubach [*pushes the Captain away*]: Mr. Chief Attorney, how can you just put up with such treatment!

Captain [*imitating her*]: Mr. Chief Attorney, Mr. Chief Attorney! How can you put up with people like us! You're really much too good for us!

K [*goes closer to Miss Bürstner, stands right in front of her*]: Miss Bürstner, I'm speaking only to you. I want to tell you something. There's something in my life—something like an unending struggle. . . . No, there are times of waiting in between, in fact it's mostly waiting—and then comes the struggle, then come the blows; and then I'm waiting again . . .

[*Miss Bürstner breaks into laughter that sounds more like despairing sobs. She stands in the doorway shaking from this fit. Mrs. Grubach has pushed the Captain to the door. She first pushes Miss Bürstner back, then shoves the Captain out and shuts the door behind herself. K remains standing motionless.*]

Scene 7

[*The dim light makes everything in the room appear gray and leaden. K drags himself to the bed, sinks down on it. After a while faint sounds are heard from outside. A ring, steps, unintelligible voices. A call from Miss Bürstner. A door is closed. Then the voices are closer. What they say cannot be understood, but they sound very close. A low male voice, Miss Bürstner's laughter. K puts his ear next to the wall; sits there, bolt upright.*]

Clear, yet still unrecognizable sounds. Perhaps a giggling, perhaps a whispering, heavy breathing, panting. Yet it could also be a scraping and scratching of objects being pushed around. A kind of grinding or groaning can be heard.

The sounds continue. They derive from an effort, an overpowering and agonizing effort that is totally strange. K presses his ear against the wall, his mouth is open. Darkness.]

Scene 8

[In the office. K is at his desk. Papers are spread in front of him. Enter the Director and the Public Prosecutor. The Director is an older man with a smile that is like a tic. From time to time he bares his teeth in a flash. The Public Prosecutor is very portly. They go up to K, who rises.]

Director: I'm here with Mr. Hasterer . . .

Public Prosecutor [embraces K]: My dear boy!

[K frees himself from the embrace.]

Director: The public prosecutor thought . . .

Public Prosecutor: Off duty! I'm off duty!

Director: To me you're always the public prosecutor [bares his teeth] . . . Your suggestions are always of the greatest value. And this time you spoke from the soul when you said he should be promoted. [To K, with his smile] . . . Indeed, your talents are not properly utilized here . . .

K: But sir, I really feel at home here. I couldn't achieve anything better elsewhere.

Director: Always modest, always modest! You've no idea what you could truly make of yourself. You're to be transferred to corporate headquarters. There you'll have real possibilities for development!

K: Sir, at the moment I'm working on so many cases that I want to follow through on. The responsibility I've assumed . . .

Director: That's just it! Few people in our company are as conscious of their responsibility as you. And on that I'm at one with the public prosecutor when he says, the more responsible a person is, the greater his responsibility should be. How few there are who have what it takes to lead, to direct! How long have you actually been in this office?

K: Two years, sir. And before . . .

Director: Yes, yes, I know. When you came to us as a young lawyer, to our legal department, I could see right away—the future belongs to him, he has that open gaze . . .

Public Prosecutor: Not for nothing did he study with me!

K: Sir, I don't know whether I can accept your offer. At headquarters . . . no, I don't belong at headquarters.

Public Prosecutor: But Josef! You're just right for headquarters. That's where you'll be in your true element. Even as a young man you were raving to me about how you wanted to know the world. And I told your father, that Josef, he's got greatness in him!

K: Mr. Hasterer, things right here are already too big, too complex . . .

Director: I know, I know! It's been tough for you in recent days. How could I have left you in the lurch like that? [*The Smile.*] Would you like us to provide you with a new apartment?

K: No, no absolutely not. I'm very comfortable in the apartment; to move now would be impossible!

Director: And Mr. Hasterer reminded me that yesterday was your birthday. How could I forget that! [*Takes an envelope from his breast pocket, hands it to K.*] Here's an appreciation! OK, next week you'll wind up all current matters and make sure Mr. Kaminer understands the job—he'll be taking your place. The sooner you come on over to us, the better! [*The Director leaves. The Public Prosecutor draws up a chair, sits down. K takes his place again at the desk.*]

Public Prosecutor: I managed that well, didn't I? Aren't you glad about the promotion? It also means a salary increase.

K: I don't need more . . .

Public Prosecutor: One always needs more!

K: Mr. Hasterer, you know that I didn't really want to leave the legal department. With legal questions, you know where you stand. Everything is structured. And then you advised me to go over to insurance. You said there would be paragraphs and laws there too. But everything was more elastic . . .

Public Prosecutor: More fluid, hence more interesting . . .

K: I had to learn to read the truth in people's faces. All I had to rely on was my own intuition. After two years I'm finally able to judge whether someone's speaking the truth . . .

Public Prosecutor: My boy, that's why you're no longer in the right place. Studying faces—that diverts you.

K: I'm finding out about myself. I've discovered what I want and what I'm good for. Mr. Hasterer, for me the move to headquarters is really out of the question.

Public Prosecutor: You can't do that to the director!

K: Mr. Hasterer, were you in my apartment yesterday?

Public Prosecutor: Excuse me?

K: Sir, how is it that you have such influence on the director?

Public Prosecutor: Well, dear boy, I know a thing or two. I have some things under my control. The director has no choice but to listen to my advice. Later you'll understand all that. But to do so you'll need more insight. Josef, I've followed your career. You have the capacity to formulate and summarize issues. Your monthly reports are of high ethical value. One could almost say they're like poetry. At any rate they're too good for a sub-department. They should benefit the whole enterprise. Your idealism—we could use more of that!

K: Mr. Hasterer . . .

Public prosecutor: Why do you address me so formally? We've been on intimate terms since the old days . . .

[The Public Prosecutor has risen to his feet. At that moment the telephone on the desk rings. K lifts the receiver. The Public Prosecutor waves to K and leaves. He walks slowly, in order to hear a bit more of the conversation.]

K: On Sunday? . . . Your letter? Yes, I received it . . . Where? . . . No, I don't drive . . . No, I don't own a car . . . A taxi? No . . . It's in a suburb? . . . Past the freight depot? That's quite a way . . . No, I won't take a taxi . . . on Julius Street, yes . . . So early? . . . Yes, I'll come . . . Yes, at nine o'clock.

[He hangs up, remains sitting motionless for a while. Does not notice the Public Prosecutor's departure. Stage suddenly dark.]

Scene 9

[The room in the boardinghouse. Again brightly lit. K enters quickly from the side. Miss Bürstner is sitting on a chair near the front, by the oval table. The door at the rear is open. Outside Miss Montag walks past several times and looks into the room. She has a hip ailment. She walks tilted to one side, dragging one leg behind. As she walks she thrusts her arms out ahead of her. K walks to and fro in the room. Miss Bürstner leans against the table.]

Miss Bürstner: And what do you think you can get from me? What's your stake? How much are you ready to cough up?

K: I don't understand. I expect nothing . . .

Miss Bürstner: Do you know what kind of a position I have?

K: You're a secretary in the bank . . .

Miss Bürstner [*laughing*]: Really, so I'm a secretary?

K: Bookkeeper perhaps.

Miss Bürstner [*turning to the door*]: Dearest, do bring me my dressing gown!
> [*Like a swimmer Miss Montag enters, after a few moments, with the desired item. She puts the dressing gown around Miss Bürstner's shoulders.*]

Miss Montag: Do you want your slippers too?

Miss Bürstner: Yes.
> [*Miss Montag sways out the door.*]

K: Miss Bürstner, I wanted to invite you for this evening. Miss Montag is welcome to come too. To a restaurant.

Miss Bürstner: So you want to invite us? Can you afford that?

K: Miss Bürstner . . .

Miss Bürstner: So you really don't know who I am.

K: At the office you're spoken of with great respect.

Miss Bürstner: Am I indeed?
> [*Miss Montag comes with the slippers. She kneels awkwardly in front of Miss Bürstner, pulls off her shoes, puts on the slippers.*]

Miss Bürstner: Dearest, tell the chief attorney what sort of position I hold.

Miss Montag [*getting up*]: Miss Bürstner is head of the bank.

K [*stops*]: Head?

Miss Bürstner: You see! You too! You can't imagine that. Head. That's just not possible.

K: No one told me.

Miss Bürstner: No, no one talks about it. Sometimes I'm called chief attorney. You haven't even heard of that. As chief attorney I would hold the same rank as you. One can rise that far. That doesn't bother anyone. But head of the bank—that's kept quiet. For negotiations with other banks, however, I'm the one that's sent out. There I can shine. There I *must* shine. I render the other directors speechless. And then I can do business.

K: But why don't you claim your status yourself—don't laugh. It's not against any rules. Who could have anything against it?

Miss Bürstner: Who indeed? No one except the CEO.

K: But you have your rights.

Miss Bürstner: What rights do I have?

K: You have all the rights and duties to which you're entitled as head of the bank.

Miss Bürstner: I have the right to stroke the CEO's shoe with my foot under the table, when I'm dining at his house.

[*Miss Montag gets up in a spiral motion. She looks at Miss Bürstner with a pained expression, strokes her face, then sways out the room.*]

K: Miss Bürstner!

Miss Bürstner: You men get whatever you need. You as a bachelor are accustomed to take for yourself whatever female happens to pass by. You thought I was a mere office employee. It would have been easy to hook up with a typist.

K: Miss Bürstner, I have never treated a woman . . .

Miss Bürstner: So much the worse! Anyway, what is there to be negotiated between us?

K: Nothing, Miss Bürstner, nothing at all! You've completely misunderstood me. We work in the same company. I would have wanted to talk to you about this work. Wanted to trust you . . .

Miss Bürstner: And now you no longer trust me?

K: Now everything may be different. Now I must look at you as my superior.

Miss Bürstner: Sure, obviously I only mix with the directors!

K: I didn't mean it like that. I mean, now people might think I'm seeking to gain advantage from knowing you.

Miss Bürstner: You could transfer to another department and rise in rank there. Perhaps you could become head of it—would everything then be different again?

K: Miss Bürstner, do you know Mr. Hasterer?

Miss Bürstner: Who doesn't know him?

K: I'm to be transferred to headquarters. I would have liked to talk to you about that. I don't want to go to headquarters.

Miss Bürstner: Then come over to me in the bank! Would you like to work under me?

K: I would like to stay in the insurance division.

Miss Bürstner: You know, it annoys me to see how you always act as if you were really ambitious, and then you don't move from the spot you're in. Sure, you're a cultured man. You surround yourself with books and art. When people walk into your room, they become almost reverential. Has he read all that, they wonder, has he studied all that. And in the daytime he works just like the rest of us. Yes, I almost admired you for having the strength to do those things after work. I just never had the time for it.

K: You also have a greater responsibility than I do. In the evening after our office closes you surely have many more discussions . . .

Miss Bürstner: There we are again! Talking about my plans. As for all this [*she points around the room*], it's as if it's worth far more than your work in the business. During the day you really only do trivial things. You don't want to rise professionally. You don't want to become head of the department. Because you despise all that. Because you—belong right here. Tell me, what do you really do here? Sometimes it seems eerie to me—no, I feel disgusted—when I hear you moving about in here at night . . .

K: These books, these pictures . . . they help me cope, deal with my weakness . . .

Miss Bürstner: Would you like to be . . . an artist yourself?

K: I don't know if I could . . .

Miss Bürstner: If you were one, what would you create?

K: I don't know. If I knew, then perhaps I'd be able to do it . . .

Miss Bürstner: What is it about art that attracts you?

K: The other . . .

Miss Bürstner: What other?

K: The thing that's different from everything around us. But which is in the middle of it.

Miss Bürstner: Like death?

K: Yes, like death. Death is like life. It's greater than we are. It outlives us. [*Miss Bürstner stands up. She stands directly in front of K. Outside Miss Montag is seen passing by the door.*]

Miss Bürstner: Kiss me then!

K: I can't.

Miss Bürstner [*bursting out into violent laughter*]: He can't! You with your weaknesses! Take a look at Miss Montag instead! How I love her infirmities!

[She hurries to the door, her laughter continuing.]

K: No, don't cry like that again!

[The door closes. Gloomy darkness filters in.]

Scene 10

[The corner of a meeting room in a warehouse. Wooden pillars. Boxes and planks as benches. The audience facing diagonally toward the dark background. Most people in their Sunday best. But some also look poor, broken down. Among the audience sits the family (from the insurance scene), as well as Franz and Willem. As K hurries in from the side, applause is just breaking out. A few people in the front rows turn to look at him but promptly turn back toward the invisible speaker. K remains standing in the foreground.]

The Party Speaker [through the loudspeaker]: So now it's up to us to bring about a change. We've had enough of the politicians' incompetence. It's time to begin something completely new! [Brief, somewhat weaker applause. The address is over. Some stand up, others stay sitting, discussing among themselves. Medley of voices. Only in the front can one gradually perceive who in a given group is speaking.]

First Voice: Yes, progress . . . people don't think nearly enough about . . .

Second Voice: Progress . . .

First Voice: What such words mean . . .

Second Voice: It means moving forward . . .

First Voice: Yes, moving forward . . .

Second Voice: But from where . . .

Third Voice: From where . . .

First Voice: From where the politicians stop moving . . .

Third Voice: But he's a politician himself . . .

Fourth Voice: He said something about rising up . . .

Second Voice: Rising up . . .

Third Voice: But not rising up like rebelling . . .

First Voice: With fighting in the streets and all . . .

Second Voice: More like a whatchamacallit . . .

First Voice: A spiritual rising up . . .

Third Voice: You'd have to give these words . . .

Second Voice: A new meaning . . .

First Voice: Think more with feelings . . . how did he put it . . .

Second Voice: Feeling, that's the true voice of reason . . .

Scene 10: First meeting in the warehouse

Fourth Voice: And in us it's been distorted . . .

First Voice: By the politicians . . . the technocrats . . . the experts . . .

Second Voice: Say what you feel . . .

Fifth Voice: I feel that I'm hungry . . .

First Voice: You mustn't spend your time just on the material questions . . .

Fourth Voice: No — on things like faith . . . justice . . . love of humanity . . .

Third Voice: But they talk about those things in the other parties too . . .

Fourth Voice: Recently . . . in the Equality Party . . .

Franz: Willem!

Willem: I'm here, Franz!

Third Voice: In the Brotherhood Party they talk of truth . . . hope . . .

First Voice: It's true that he laid into the experts . . .

Second Voice: Parasites, he called them . . .

Third Voice: Who are spreading everywhere . . .

Second Voice: Who think they're so special because they've studied something . . .

Fourth Voice: And peace . . . they talk about peace, peace above all . . .

Fifth Voice: It's always primarily about peace . . .

Fourth Voice: And it sounds like a threat . . .

Fifth Voice: Yes, watch out that you don't lose the peace . . .

Third Voice: They want to make us afraid.

Second Voice: They say we don't know which way to turn because of all the dangers . . .

Fourth Voice: So that we'll be docile . . .

Fifth Voice: And then they talk about cutbacks . . .

Fourth Voice: Yeah, cutbacks . . .

Third Voice: Why are fewer and fewer people needed . . .

Second Voice: While more and more is being produced . . .

Fifth Voice: The others decide that . . .

Second Voice: What others . . .

Fifth Voice: Well, the ones who see further than we do . . . who have the big picture . . . it has to do with the business climate . . . with the market.

First Voice: He's probably from the Revolutionary Party . . .

Third Voice: The Revolutionary Party has also gone bust . . .

Second Voice: How are we to know if this is the right party . . .

> [The Party Speaker has stepped out from the background. He is simply dressed, wears a leather jacket.]

Party Speaker: It is the right party. Why? Because it speaks to all levels of society. It doesn't represent only one particular group or class. No! It responds to all who are no longer resigned to the present state of things. The party's success can be seen in the range of people assembled here. Look around you! We have all kinds here. Wage laborers, craftsmen, white-collar workers, people from the welfare office, housewives, officials . . . future directors. [He has approached K. Takes his hand, shakes it.] Unfortunately you came rather late. Much too late. You heard hardly any of my speech.

K: It was a long way. It was difficult to find the street.

Party Speaker: You should have gotten up earlier. I suppose you're not used to getting up early? But the point is, you came. [To some bystanders] Our friend here works with the United Society for the Public Welfare.

Fourth Voice: I was ruined by them!

Party Speaker [pointing to K]: You see—the fact that people like him find their way to us proves the correctness of our program. Renewal, as we mean it, can only happen when it answers to the desires and needs of everyone. We know that we have to live together, that we're all connected—connected by our love of peace. And if we now show the politicians how numerous we are . . .

Second Voice: How are we to show that?

Party Speaker: By making the party strong! Become members! You can sign up over there [*he points to a table in the background where a secretary is sitting*] . . . there you'll get the membership book!

Third Voice: Can anyone become a member?

Party Speaker: Anyone! We make no distinctions. Young or old. Rich or poor.

Third Voice: What does it cost?

Party Speaker: You can afford it. Less than a movie ticket.

Third Voice: And what do we get for it?

Party Speaker: What you yourselves achieve. You're the ones that make the party. That's progress. Nothing is done for you here, you must do it yourselves. Everything comes from you. That's what rising up means.

[*K puts his hand over his eyes, looks for a support with his other hand. Sits down on a box. The Woman who was in his office comes up to him. Her relatives follow her. They crowd around him.*]

The Husband: What's wrong with him?

The Woman: Yes, he's the one from the insurance. [*To K*] Don't you feel well?

K: It's so hot . . . I can't get any air . . .

The Woman [*unbuttons his collar, pats his cheek, turns to the others*]: He promised us an apartment—he's very ready to help.

Third Voice: I need an apartment too!

The Woman: Leave him alone now!

[*Most of the people now leave. The breakup of the group is slow and indecisive. Some still approach the small table, leaf distractedly through the brochures, a few sign up, produce money, receive a book. The Party Speaker remains conversing with a group in the background. In the distance a few voices can be heard.*]

Second Voice: Has Willem gone already . . .

Fourth Voice: He's over there . . . with Franz . . .

Party Speaker: Would anyone else like to sign up . . .

First Voice: Are you coming to fetch the potatoes . . .

[*In the foreground the Woman and her family are also preparing to leave.*]

The Woman: We must go now . . .

K: Stay a while . . . no . . . it doesn't help . . .

[*The Woman and her relatives leave. A few stragglers continue to pass by.*]

Third Voice: Well, really . . . what a Sunday. The one free day we have and the morning's already shot . . . it's too late to start anything in the afternoon . . . we should have made use of the whole day . . .

[*The stage is now empty except for a few obscure shapes in the background. Darkness.*]

Scene 11

[*The room in the boardinghouse. Illumination comes only from the little lamp on the night table. The door in the background is open. K sits down on the bed. Outside Miss Montag can be seen from time to time. She is dragging suitcases and bundles. K stands up, goes to the door.*]

K: Mrs. Grubach!

[*Mrs. Grubach appears and comes toward him. She is carrying a few plates and a folded tablecloth.*]

Mrs. Grubach: I'm coming.

K: What's going on out there?

Mrs. Grubach: Miss Montag is moving.

K: Is she leaving?

Mrs. Grubach: No, she's moving in with Miss Bürstner.

[*Mrs. Grubach comes all the way into the room. In the semi-darkness she begins to set the table.*]

K: Why?

Mrs. Grubach: Miss Bürstner is always so afraid at night. And she wants to have Miss Montag with her then.

[*The Captain too appears outside. He helps Miss Montag carry the luggage. During the following he is seen successively with a cabin trunk, a chest of drawers, an easy chair, and a standing lamp. Miss Bürstner appears occasionally but is not involved with the move. She stops only briefly and peers into K's room.*]

K: But Miss Bürstner's room is quite small. Not big enough for two.

Mrs. Grubach: Miss Montag's bed is very narrow. Really just a camp bed you can fold up.

K: But she's bringing the rest of her furniture too. I was never in Miss Bürstner's room, so I don't know what's there. But when I think of the hallway outside, of the corridor and the toilet, then I can't imagine the room as anything but cramped. [*Mrs. Grubach leaves the room, he calls after her*] . . . It must be right in the corner by the house next door . . .

Mrs. Grubach [*turning as she walks*]: It's large enough. What's more, I think it's good that Miss Bürstner is no longer alone.

K: What does Miss Montag do, actually?

Mrs. Grubach: Miss Montag is always at home.

K: How can you know that . . . you're often gone yourself . . .

Mrs. Grubach: Miss Montag is always there when I leave. And she's there when I come back.

K: But in the meantime—what happens in the meantime?

[*Mrs. Grubach has disappeared. K runs after her, stops by the door. The Captain comes by with a wastepaper basket filled with a variety of objects.*]

Captain [*turns to K*]: Won't you give us a hand? No—you're always only a spectator.

[*Mrs. Grubach returns, with place settings and a carafe.*]

K: Mrs. Grubach, do you know what Miss Bürstner's position is?

Mrs. Grubach [*setting the table*]: You mean her corporate position? That she's head of the bank? You think it doesn't fit her rank for her to share her room? But that's what she wants . . .

K: Look, I've lived here such a long time, and I'm still not entirely clear about the layout of the rooms in this boardinghouse. And yet it's always very important to me to know what my immediate environment looks like. The captain's room . . .

[*Only now does he notice that Mrs. Grubach meanwhile has gone out again. Waits a few moments until she returns. She carries a bowl of soup that she puts down on the table. Her movements at the table are, in the semi-darkness, barely discernible.*]

K: As I was saying . . . the room of Mr. Lanz . . .

Mrs. Grubach: Were you never in there with my nephew?

K: No. . . . Is he actually your sister's or your brother's son?

Mrs. Grubach: In fact he was my sister's foster son. He came to me as a child, when my sister died shortly after the war . . . the last war . . . wouldn't you like to eat?

K [*sitting down*]: So your nephew was already with you as a child . . . and then?

Mrs. Grubach: He was with me until his military service. He was like a son to me. And then when he'd become a captain and was allowed to live off the base, he came back to us — yes, my husband was still living then . . . [*She sits down at the table. K picks up the spoon but doesn't eat.*]

Mrs. Grubach: Eat up now!

K: Really, we could be like a family, since you said that I'd been like a son to your husband.

Mrs. Grubach: Did I say that?

K: The captain and I — brothers. Yes, mother Grubach — I've often wanted to call you that.

Mrs. Grubach: And your own parents?

K: I never see them.

Mrs. Grubach [*shakes her head*]: So you have to seek out other parents . . .

K: You know, that family stuff, growing up with parents and siblings — it's really nothing but a damned nuisance. You live crammed together, never get free of one another. I left home to find my own way. But it was immensely difficult for me. I admit it. I admit it, Mrs. Grubach, I find it very difficult to cope with my life. Do you understand me?

Mrs. Grubach: The soup's getting cold.

K [*eats some spoonfuls of soup, puts the spoon down again*]: You see, in my profession I deal with vastly complicated matters that always have a direct impact on other people's lives. For a long time I simply did my work. And then suddenly that wasn't enough. Since then I've wanted to know the consequences of everything I do — and I wonder what lies behind everything that influences me . . .

[*Outside in the hall, voices are heard again. Miss Bürstner and the Captain appear, laughing. The Captain puts on his military cap, Miss Bürstner adjusts her hat. Mrs. Grubach stands up.*]

K: Do stay a while, Mrs. Grubach.

Mrs. Grubach: But then you must promise me to eat up.

[*Mrs. Grubach sits down again. K eats slowly, reluctantly. The Captain and Miss Bürstner have gone away. The outer door to the apartment is opened and slammed shut.*]

K: How am I to understand what goes on in the world when I can't grasp the meaning of everything that happens right here. Today I was at a political meeting. It was doubtless all about things that are important for our lives, but I just couldn't take in any of it. I felt helpless . . .

Mrs. Grubach: Oh, that's nothing special. I always feel like that when I'm among lots of people . . .

K: But it's precisely when one is together with many people that one should grasp more than a single individual can. One should be able to see what really counts. I had thought, now a meaning would be revealed. My work alone just isn't enough for me any more . . .

Mrs. Grubach: Yes, perhaps you're in the wrong place. Perhaps you should do something quite different . . .

K [*suddenly eating with eagerness*]: Yes—yes, Mrs. Grubach. What you say encourages me. I really will reach a solution. There, just for a moment, I sensed that a solution exists. And that's already a lot! I'm going to go after it immediately . . .

[*Has put down the spoon and jumped to his feet. Hurries out of the room. Darkness.*]

Scene 12

[*In the office. Only K's desk is illuminated. K comes running in from the side. Rabensteiner sits at K's desk. The objects on the desk are in a mess. All the drawers are pulled out. Rabensteiner is sifting through papers and reading letters; he pays no attention to K's arrival.*]

K: What are you doing there?

Rabensteiner: I? What do you mean? I have to put things in order for your successor.

K: But that's my concern.

Rabensteiner: I just want to save you the trouble. You're expected tomorrow in corporate headquarters. You'll have plenty to do there.

K: But I haven't made up my mind yet!

Rabensteiner: On the contrary! Miss Bürstner said you'd made up your mind.

K: Miss Bürstner?

Rabensteiner: Yes. Today. I telephone—there's no chief attorney in the boardinghouse. The chief attorney already left, at seven in the morning. And where to? To a political meeting. Really! Well, now. . . . But we your colleagues, we're working all day Sunday; we've been preparing your future activities. Myself, the director, and the head of the bank. We've set up your entire work sphere. You'll hit the ground running. A secretary will be at your disposal.

K: But . . .

Rabensteiner: No buts! There are no buts at headquarters. [*K picks up a few* things from the surface of the desk, puts them in order. Looks absently at one of the photographs.]

Rabensteiner: These things, you're probably discarding them?

K: No!

Rabensteiner: Then you're taking them home?

K: No . . .

Rabensteiner: You surely don't want to take them with you to the new office.

K: I certainly do!

Rabensteiner: Then Willem and Franz will move them for you . . .

K: Willem and Franz?

Rabensteiner: They're waiting here.

[K looks around uncertainly. A muted grunting and groaning, suppressed cries can be heard. Also a smacking sound, as on bare skin.]

K: Where?

Rabensteiner: In the storeroom. They're passing the time.

K: The storeroom?

Rabensteiner: In the storeroom for files.

[The crunch of wood breaking. A cry. In the background the door of a narrow storeroom swings open. There, for a few seconds, in the garish light, are to be seen Willem, Franz, and Miss Bürstner. All three appear to be naked, smeared with blood. They are writhing around together. The door slams shut again. K stands staring into the darkness. The desk lamp is extinguished.]

ACT TWO

Scene 13

[*In the new office. Only one desk. But it is the same desk as before. The objects on it are also arranged in their old order. Near the desk a low table with a few comfortable armchairs. Instead of the city plans, there are now maps of the earth. Lines connect the capital cities directly across continents and seas. K sits bolt upright at his desk.*]

Rabensteiner: Punctual. Good.

K: You're here too?

Rabensteiner: I'm here too.

K: I stopped by Kaminer's office. Wanted to explain a few cases to him. He said he knew about everything.

Rabensteiner: Dealt with everything yesterday. He had been in on everything for a long time anyway.

K: How is he to understand things that have cost me years of work?

Rabensteiner: But you know that we've introduced the new system. The simplified procedures mean that what used to require a sizable team can now be accomplished by just a few workers. You yourself had become superfluous. You with your card files . . .

K: It's those card files that matter to me. They bring the human beings behind the particular case closer to me . . .

Rabensteiner: Everything can be accessed by the new system. My dear fellow, you were our museum piece!

K: One must listen to everyone, Mr. Rabensteiner, one must talk with everyone . . .

Rabensteiner: Certainly! People are our central concern. Our reputation is based on that, after all. Yes, you are always full of understanding. But you also made too many commitments. You didn't content yourself with the prescribed friendliness. You made too many promises. That was the mistake.

K: Insurance was our most respected undertaking. We were known for our personal involvement with our clients . . .

Rabensteiner: Are not our bank, our apartment building, our transportation project just as respected? You were given plenty of leeway. But although you're very good at calculation, the deficit grew steadily on your watch. You react to the slightest discordant note—but the losses . . . I suppose they didn't bother you at all?

K: I insist that I be kept informed concerning the affairs of the insurance department, that I receive responses to my inquiries . . .

Rabensteiner: But of course! That's why you've moved to headquarters— to broaden your perspective. There you'll have all the departments at your beck and call . . .

[The Director has entered. With his sudden, distorted smile he goes up to K, who rises. The Director shakes his hand.]

Director: I see you're already hard at work. That's as it should be. When you've thoroughly examined the papers, you can take your tour of the facilities. Your secretary will escort you. Mr. Hasterer is also already waiting to confer with you. People don't just rush in on you here—it isn't done. Are you ready to receive Mr. Hasterer?

[K remains silent.]

Rabensteiner: That's really important: never forget the role of the outer office. It's the job of people there to take the pressure off you. [By the speaker on the desk a small light flashes. K doesn't move. Rabensteiner presses the button.]

Voice through the speaker: May Mr. Hasterer come in now?

Rabensteiner: Yes, please!

[As the Director and Rabensteiner leave, the Public Prosecutor enters, accompanied by a woman.]

Scene 14

[The Public Prosecutor goes up to K with open arms, embraces him. The woman remains standing at a distance.]

Public Prosecutor: I'd like to present to you your secretary.

[The woman goes up to K, greets him, then sits down on one of the armchairs. Her attitude is quiet and attentive. The Public Prosecutor presses K down onto his

Scene 14: Public Prosecutor, K, Leni

chair; *he himself sits down on the desk, in the process pushing the objects arranged there to one side.*]

K: Why are you bringing me the secretary?

Public Prosecutor: Don't be so formal, Josef! You know, I was visiting your parents and told them the news!

K: What news . . .

Public Prosecutor: About your promotion.

K: Oh, that's nothing . . .

Public Prosecutor: How proud your father was! He's so ill and almost always in bed . . . but he leaped up and ran around the room in his nightshirt . . . [*roaring with laughter*] . . . Oh, that I'm alive to hear that, he shouted. If you knew how he loves you, you, his only son! And . . . [*he bends over K and puts his hand on his shoulder.*]

K: And?

Public Prosecutor: Aren't you going to ask after your mother?

K: My mother . . .

Public Prosecutor: She's blind. Your mother has gone blind.

K: Blind . . .

Public Prosecutor: A year ago. But she's forgiven you . . .

K: Forgiven what . . .

Public Prosecutor: That you deserted her. That you've never returned home. That you've never sent her any news.

K: What should I have . . .

Public Prosecutor: Can't you imagine what it means for parents to lose their son, always to have to ask others how he's doing, what he's doing. . . . It's really time for you to visit them . . .

K: I can't do that . . .

Public Prosecutor: But Josef! Think how important cohesion is for a family. You're the one who always talks about mutual understanding, about the need to listen to others, to help others . . .

K: That wasn't possible there any more . . .

Public Prosecutor: Wrong, Josef, wrong! You're the one who was needed, you with your insights into things!

K: My insights were what drove us apart. Whenever I saw how things were in the world and wanted to talk about it, they pushed me away. Don't get us mixed up in that, they said . . .

Public Prosecutor: No, they suffered with you! How often did I hear your father say, what am I to do with Josef—he says he despairs of everything!

K: They forbade me to visit the poor districts . . .

Public Prosecutor: You were still a child. They were afraid of what might happen.

K: I was told to play with a boy who frightened me and was not allowed to spend time with a girl I liked. Because the boy came from a wealthy household while the girl's parents were destitute . . .

Public Prosecutor: They wanted security!

K: Yes! They wanted to be secure, respectable. They wanted to keep disaster at a distance—so they attracted it! Disaster is vengeful: whoever fears and denies it, that's who it seeks out. In the end it became part of us, every word was stamped by it . . . yes, there was also some tenderness and gentleness . . .

Public Prosecutor: And that's when you should have provided comfort!

K: I? But the disaster was written all over me . . . I could see what was really happening . . .

Public Prosecutor: I don't understand what you mean, Josef!

K: What I mean! I mean the way people everywhere were persecuted, hunted down, massacred . . .

Public Prosecutor: Yes, yes, but all that isn't happening here! That's all far away from us. That's no reason for us to worry.

K: It's pressing upon us all the time . . .

Public Prosecutor: But my boy, really! We can't live like that. The fact that somewhere people are still hungry, that doesn't have to spoil our appetite. That there's destruction going on somewhere doesn't have to take away our pleasure in building something. I fully respect your concerns! But you help no one with your laments about the general misery. Help with improvements in your immediate circle. Now you have the opportunity. You've done right to obtain an influential position for yourself. Only the person with influence can intervene and change things. Cheerfulness, my boy! Cheerfulness is what's needed now. The whole world is opening to you [he points to the world maps] — sure, there are pockets of poverty here and there, big pockets even, you're right about that — but now it's your role to illuminate them, you're one of the pioneers, the new colonizers! Yes, a new colonization has begun — a spiritual colonization, no violence, no, never with violence — an economic colonization combined with spiritual power — you belong to the new elite!

K: I can't see myself that way . . .

Public Prosecutor: You'll learn to do so. That's how it is with all knowledge. One discovery leads to the next. You've never been obtuse. I remember how effortlessly you moved from natural law to commercial law, how purposefully you worked in the insurance department; I hardly need to tell you that, you know your own capacities, you just sometimes let yourself be distracted by this tendency, a tendency I'm convinced you'll soon cast off — and your secretary will help you do so . . .

[The Secretary gets up, takes a few steps toward the desk. The Public Prosecutor gets down ponderously from his perch. K also stands up.]

Public Prosecutor: I hand you over to her . . .

[The Public Prosecutor leaves. The Secretary goes up to the desk, rearranges the displaced objects in their proper order.]

K: I didn't catch your name . . .

Secretary: Call me Leni.

[Darkness.]

Scene 15

[*The office is brightly lit. K alone at the desk. Willem and Franz enter in civilian clothes. They place a stack of papers on the desk.*]

K: Are you here now?

Willem: We were promoted too. I'm employed at headquarters.

Franz: And I'm in the bank.

Willem: Miss Bürstner thinks a lot of Franz.

Franz: Don't I fit in there? Do you think I'm stupid?

K: Why should I think you stupid?

Franz: I know you think most people stupid.

K: I do?

Franz: I noticed that. A month ago. When we were at your place because of the vent. You heard something we couldn't hear.

Willem: I'm still of the opinion that there's nothing wrong.

Franz: The director said there must be something wrong if you say so, and that everyone is stupid who doesn't understand what you mean.

K: But if you were promoted, that means people can't think you're stupid.

Willem: We could have been fired.

Franz: Yes, at first it looked as though we'd be fired.

Willem: There must be some reason why we weren't fired.

K: You're competent workers. You'll be divisional leaders one day.

Willem: Yes! [*Raises his index finger.*] Now I've got it! You and I and everyone else, we're always being transferred. I began as a messenger in transportation. Then moved to construction. And then to maintenance.

Franz: And Miss Bürstner began in our travel office. Then she was a typist in production. Then cashier in the bank. Now she's a bookkeeper there.

Willem: And you—you began in the legal advice office. Then in insurance. Soon you'll probably be on the board. Or somewhere else . . .

K: Somewhere else?

Willem: Well, I'm not saying you'll become a window cleaner or floor sweeper—but I know someone who was an engineer and is now a stoker.

K: Mr. Willem, do you think I'm not suited for my position?

Willem: No one's better suited! It's just these things there on your desk. I don't know, they look so funny to me. As if the desk were not here but somewhere else. This guy with the old-fashioned cap and the mustache [*he points to one of the photos*] — what's he got to do with administration? I'm only asking, I don't understand anything about it.

K: He was a miner.

Franz: Was he your grandfather?

K: No, he was someone . . . who built himself a palace.

Willem: A palace?

K: Not a real palace. A palace deep underground. With promenades and galleries and pillars. Everything upside down. Staircases down to the top of the tower. Everything made of clay. He worked it with his hands. The walls all decorated. Stones pressed into them and lumps of coal and . . .

Franz: Did he live there?

K: No, he couldn't live there . . .

Willem: To build a palace and then not to live in it . . .

K: He lived in a hut nearby. But he spent all his free time inside his construction. His whole life. Was always making it better and more beautiful . . .

Franz: And everything upside down . . .

K: Everything rising downward. You couldn't see it from outside. And he built a monument for himself too . . . a vault . . .

Willem [*bending over another photo*]: Is it this hole here, with the railing?

[*Rabensteiner has entered from the side. On tiptoe he approaches K from behind. At the same time Willem and Franz leave.*]

Scene 16

[*Rabensteiner has sneaked up close to K.*]

Rabensteiner: I hear you talking about stones and graves.

K [*turning in surprise*]: No, about art. I am to direct the art association, so I thought it good to prepare the ground a bit, to stimulate the aesthetic senses.

Rabensteiner: But the art association is not supposed to take up employees' time during working hours. You're the exception, of course. You have to carry out the purchase of artworks. To select the appropriate walls for them in the offices. Yes, it's your job to worry about beauty. To add something light and pleasant to the atmosphere, so to speak. That then has its effect on everyone.

K: Mr. Rabensteiner, I've been thinking about something. The fact is, none of us has a firm position here. If someone begins to get used to a particular workplace, he gets moved on elsewhere . . .

Rabensteiner: Correct! We all move around!

K: But we don't decide to do that ourselves. We simply get shifted from here to there.

Rabensteiner: Because work activity is to stimulate the whole person. What the individual often doesn't understand—he's then pushed to do so by management. Thus all the employee's talents can be utilized. And this goes not only for practical tasks, it applies to one's whole attitude toward work. I'd call it a revolutionary approach . . .

K: Yes, perhaps I do feel freer now myself. Yes! I'm beginning to see the whole . . . the overall project . . .

Rabensteiner: Even the director has noticed that you've succeeded in switching over in just a few weeks. And perhaps you'd also be ready soon to exchange your shabby boardinghouse room for something . . . a little more prestigious?

K: Oh no, I want to stay where I am!

Rabensteiner: Is the sound gone now?

K: No!

[Rabensteiner leaves. Darkness.]

Scene 17

[The corner of the meeting room in the shed. The background is dark. Visitors come one at a time and in small groups. Some sit down on the boxes and benches, others stand around. A murmur of voices. Now and then individual words become clear. Only the foreground is illuminated. K and Leni are sitting there on a bench.]

K: We went to the Freedom Party, to the Equality Party . . . which party is it today?

Leni: The Revolutionary Party . . . or rather, one section of it.

K: Which one?

Leni: You never know that in advance.

K: But so many people come anyway . . .

Leni: That's just it: the fact that nothing is fixed is what attracts most people.

K: There were lots of police outside . . .

Fourth Voice: Water cannons were just around the corner . . .

Leni: The police are always there when there's uncertainty. The more du-
bious a meeting, the more police show up.

K: The previous time, at the Progressive Party meeting, I didn't notice
any surveillance at all—yet plenty of subversive matters were talked
about.

Leni: The stuff about the people rising up. But the people aren't expected
to rise up themselves. They are to be raised up. Behind the Progressive
Party there are official networks from the education system.

K: As far as I could understand, the talk there was also against education,
against educated people . . .

Leni: But that's normal. A fishing line with a hook is first thrown out.
The ones who are supposed to bite are those who at least know that
they know nothing. The ones who feel themselves to be cheated. Who
think there are others who know more than themselves. These others
then, the ones who know more, are denounced. That they know
something you the audience doesn't know—that's reprehensible.
They must have obtained such knowledge illegitimately. The person
hooked by this line of talk is hungry and—above all—hangs around
restlessly. The ones who don't bite, who don't become agitated—
there's no point fishing for them. And to the ones who are on your
line, you can say, now it's your turn. Now there's something you can
learn. And the first thing they learn is to despise the kind of education
from which they were excluded.

K: But if you are to rise higher, you must have something ahead of you
that's enticing . . .

Leni: The bait is already lodged in their throats.

K: Are they to choke on it, then?

Leni: They're not supposed to notice it. The barb is stuck in the roof of
the mouth and they are pulled upwards. Finally they're in open air.

K: What kind of air! Can they breathe there?

Leni: They are human. They're driven together. To a meeting.

K: They've come on their own accord . . . willingly . . .

Leni: Have they?

K: All these people . . . unease is driving them . . . something unfulfilled
. . . they want to get together, to improve their lot . . .

Leni: They've been lured here. Lured together with everything that torments them. Either the housing shortage or too high rents. Either poverty or excessive taxes. Either idleness or overwork. Either loneliness or family crises. They are made completely empty. And then they wait for someone to say something to them. And when they get to know just a little bit about how things are, they believe they know everything. But the terrible thing is . . .

K: Terrible?

Leni: They don't expect enlightenment, they expect . . . kindness.

[The Woman whom K knows appears in the crowd. Her family accompanies her. They sit down near K. The Woman does not seem to have recognized K yet. He turns away quickly.]

The Woman: Do you think that woman will speak today?

The Husband: Do you mean the bandy-legged one?

The Woman: I don't know . . . she limps . . .

The Husband: Perhaps that's why so many women are here . . .

[The seated people become restless. Hands point to the background, where nothing can be seen. A microphone is tested. A voice counts: one, two, three. New arrivals push forward, looking for seating.]

K: But it's a basic urge, thinking. How can others who think prevent people from thinking . . .

Leni: They don't prevent them, they teach them to think in a particular way.

[Someone sitting nearby, the Fifth Voice, joins the conversation. The Woman and her relatives also turn toward K and Leni. K leans backward in order to conceal himself.]

Fifth Voice: Right! They always want to teach us stuff that's got nothing whatever to do with us.

Third Voice: Aren't you in the Revolutionary Party?

Fifth Voice: The most revolutionary thing nowadays is to look at one's own condition.

The Woman: If people really looked, they'd sure see something! I clean up the filth and vomit in the toilet at the train station. Unconscious and dead people lie around there. I drag them out. Even where we live—no one else lives there anymore—they're lying around. Boozing and pumping stuff into their veins. Tarts bring in their customers. [She leans farther forward, addresses K.] And my husband, take a look at

him! [Points at the Husband, who's sitting there slumped down.] And the old
people! [Points at the Old People, who gaze ahead, their mouths wide open.]
There are my helpers . . .

K: Hasn't a new apartment been assigned to you, then?

The Woman: That's how you are! Just like the others. Promises, promises—and nothing ever happens.

K: But long ago I . . .

The Woman: Long ago they did everything for you—or else they never
heard of you!

K: I will investigate first thing tomorrow—there's been some misunder-
standing.

The Woman: Sure, always misunderstandings! How you can even run
your operation, with all the misunderstandings!

Fifth Voice: It's the misunderstandings that do it!

K: I will take care of the matter . . .

The Woman: You hear—he will take care of the matter!

[During this exchange two men have pushed through the crowd. Now and then
they grab someone, whom they quickly lead away. This activity is barely noticed
by those in attendance, indeed is hard to make out in the muted lighting. The
two men then appear in the foreground. One sees that they are Franz and Willem.
They push from behind up against the speaker of the Fifth Voice; Franz twists his
right arm roughly against his back. Willem briefly waves some identification in
front of his face. Immediately they turn him around and shove him out between
them. At the same time attention has turned to the background. The voice of the
Party Speaker resounds through the microphone.]

Party Speaker: My worthy listeners! I will tell you what is to be done . . .

The Husband: So it's not the bandy-legged woman!

[Darkness.]

Scene 18

[In the office. K at his desk. The photographs and other objects are no longer on it.
Enter the Director, the Public Prosecutor, Rabensteiner, Kaminer, and Leni. Leni
sits in the armchair. The others approach K, who gets up.]

Director: So we're about to take the great step.

Public Prosecutor: Inwardly there is ceaseless movement; outwardly we
display a unique cohesion.

K: Everyone is to commit his energies where he is needed . . .

Public Prosecutor: Democracy means freedom from all ties. Everyone should be open to everyone else.

Rabensteiner: Everyone must learn to cooperate with everyone else.

Public Prosecutor: We've developed our model on that basis.

Kaminer: The perfect community of interests . . .

Director: Our institution will stand unique in the marketplace.

K: If there is no longer any competitiveness, then selfishness is also suspended. Then we will be exclusively serving the public good.

Public Prosecutor: Not entirely, Josef! With your inventiveness you can help our group of companies to expand still further. Growth is beginning on an international scale. Why talk about cartels and trusts? Those words are out of date. The leadership of the economy is at stake. We're talking about political leadership!

Rabensteiner: We are more than a political party.

Kaminer: And art is essential to our politics.

Director [turning to K with his special smile]: And you understood all that! Precisely because of your experience in suffering. You let yourself be tormented by all the existing imperfections. You kept a constant lookout for the other possibilities — the kinder, gentler possibilities. And so we find our way to this new model, one embodying the unity of profit and self-denial, of authority and love of humanity, of art and politics — in short, the unity of reason and emotion!

Rabensteiner: Do you remember — we conversed once about the vision of a society based on reason. We had been discussing the brevity of all revolutionary experiments. Before they could come to fruition, they were destroyed or disintegrated from within, their leaders overthrown, maligned, murdered. Never had anything as stable as our system been able to establish itself.

Director [to K, with a laugh turning to a grimace]: Doubtless you'll say that we too, with our policy of constant transfers, achieve only fragmentation! People are alienated from themselves, become helpless tools in our hands!

Public Prosecutor [to K]: But the best proof that that's not the case is — you yourself! You wanted to become an artist, a poet! And you are one. In a higher sense. It is the expression of life itself that attracts you now. Now you are realizing a dream. You're working with the stuff of life itself. With the most contradictory of artistic material. You're truly inspired, a new kind of human!

K: I want to know about the whole state of things from which our project emerged. It was so well established that it's hardly changed even today.

Rabensteiner: Hasn't it changed since you were brought over to headquarters? After barely three months you're to be put on the board! What a rise!

Kaminer: You'll move to a villa! Travel! I've already set up the program! [K waves all this away with his hands. The Director, the Public Prosecutor, Rabensteiner, and Kaminer get ready to leave. The Director turns around again. His face is horribly contorted by The Smile.]

Director: The purchase of artworks is still to be done! Only you can do it! As you know, we need wall paintings for the new public reception building . . .

[Everyone leaves. Leni has gotten up, goes over to K and presses down his hands. Darkness.]

Scene 19

[In the studio of the painter Titorelli. Monumental painting all around, violently compressed images, with figurative elements. In the semi-darkness only occasional details can be discerned. Amidst them are reproductions of other works, by Uccello, Piero della Francesca, Géricault, Courbet, Diego Rivera. Also some large photographic portraits, e.g., of Kafka and Brecht.

Titorelli stands to one side. He is wearing a simple gray coverall. K and Leni wander round between the pictures.]

K: And what would happen if these pictures were to hang in our reception building?

Leni: Meaning what?

K: Would they break the place to bits, or would the place extinguish the pictures?

Leni: A fearful struggle would take place.

K: But who would win?

Leni: The pictures would win. And, in the process, lose. Because the institution must always be in the right.

K: They could have an impact on our dealings . . .

Leni: Do you still believe that?

K: I've believed it until now. That was what sustained me. I wanted to come as close as possible to the colossal strivings that are going on everywhere. Now I no longer believe it. We never get beyond a certain point. And perhaps that's where other imaginings begin, focused on something visible . . . tangible.

Titorelli: You mean art.

K: How you say that, Titorelli, with such amazing indifference. As if it were the most self-evident thing in the world. Yes . . . that's how you're able to endure life . . .

Titorelli: It endures me. My task is to oppose life. I cut around in it. Get something out of it for myself. Rip something out of life that it doesn't want to give up, that really doesn't belong to it. Something we usually just aim for but never grasp. And it's the one thing we can truly possess, totally and absolutely. It's a violent assault on life, a rape!

K: And yet . . . it points beyond itself . . .

Titorelli: You think so? It's only a substitute.

K: Substitute—for what?

Titorelli: For life itself, of course.

K: But you gain your truth *from* life . . .

Titorelli: I don't know if it's truth. Life doesn't contain a truth. I paint something as a consolation, when I can no longer keep looking at life as a whole. I sit there for hours, weeks, dozing. When I paint, I yell, shriek and sob; often because of my tears I can't see what's coming into being.

K: Is that what we call clarity?

Leni: Or beauty.

Titorelli: For me it's filth, scum, spawn of suffering. Everything bleeds. They're entrails. It's shit.

K: How can it come across like purity?

Titorelli: Because you want to see it that way.

K: No—there's something really there. It overwhelms us. [*He goes up to one of the pictures, touches it. The fresh paint sticks to his fingers. He contemplates his smeared hand.*] Now I've destroyed something of yours!

Titorelli: No! That's how I want it! Look—everywhere traces of hands. When I've sketched out a picture, I get people up from the street. People from the bar. From the harbor. Sometimes I pull a driver out of his truck, stuff money in his pocket, drag him with me, press him up against the canvas. I want everyone to participate. Often they come of their own accord. They know Titorelli! They get a brush thrust into their hands — here, this figure [*he points to a picture*] is of a sailor . . . and the two female figures here — do you recognize them? — one is a bank employee, the other a cripple . . . you see, they're naked — I pressed them into the colors . . . you see, stomach, sex, thighs — I draw their faces in while they're embracing; they cried out too, while I was weeping . . . yes . . . a single lamentation . . . wouldn't you also like . . .

K [*retreats anxiously, wipes his hands on a cloth that he's picked up off the floor*]: No . . . not yet . . .

Titorelli: Not yet? But you'd like to. You feel the urge to participate with your whole body in the depravity of art . . .

K: Is it depravity?

Titorelli: Ha! Is it depravity! You know very well what the answer is. And your lady friend knows it too. Ask her, she'll tell you.

K: Leni, do you know?

Leni: Oh, please take care! I've been assigned to guard you. I know everything about you. I know your most secret impulses. If you fall, I fall too.

K: How can you know everything about me?

Leni: You've been in the head office. Didn't you see that every detail is preserved there concerning everyone who comes even briefly into contact with the company? Every step you've taken, every one of your utterances is preserved. Even your future actions have already been calculated, based on the possibilities that lie within you.

K: And if I did something that deviated from everything that could be predicted . . .

Leni: Then you would have to become completely empty. To renounce all meaning. But it's impossible for you to give up searching for a meaning.

Titorelli: If you were to do that, you'd be where I am. It's empty here. Absolutely empty. Nothing can be predicted. But you don't dare. That's it, sir — you're afraid of what might happen to you. Leni could explain it to you better. I can't. Whenever I try, I'm overcome . . . [*He begins to sob. He grasps the brush, dips it in the paints that are squeezed out onto a newspaper, approaches one of the half-painted canvases in a corner where he can hardly be seen anymore.*]

K: Afraid? No! Right now I could easily make that move . . . I could, couldn't I, Leni . . . and perhaps it would even give me great joy; but it would be too easy . . . it's as if I would leave out something . . . and then the act itself would already be superfluous . . .

[*The painter's sobbing, the scraping and scratching of the brush can still be heard for a time. Darkness.*]

Scene 20

[*The room in the boardinghouse. Only the small bedside lamp gives off light. K enters from the side. Clambers over the table and chairs. Stumbles over piles of books, statuettes. Throws himself on the bed. The door in the background is opened. Blinding light pours in. Mrs. Grubach appears. Behind her a group of people, closely pressed together.*]

Mrs. Grubach: Here are some people who want to see you.

[*K remains stretched out on the bed. The Woman steps forward from the group. She is wrapped in a blanket, carries some bundles. Her relatives are also lugging blankets and shapeless sacks. The Woman pushes past Mrs. Grubach, enters the room.*]

The Woman: It's getting to be winter now, and still nothing has changed. I can't stay there with the children any longer.

[*K sits up. The Children enter the room. The two Old People come through the door.*]

The Old Man: We were told you were about to leave on a trip, so we thought . . .

The Old Woman: That it wouldn't disturb you, if we. . . .

Mrs. Grubach: Shall I call the police?

K [*waving this suggestion aside*]: No, no . . .

The Woman [*coming closer*]: If we could live here for a while . . .

The Husband [*stepping forward*]: We could also clean up for you . . .

The Woman: And cook . . .

The Old Woman: And do the washing . . .

Mrs. Grubach: Who are they?

K: Oh, let them in . . .

The Children: We're there already!

[*The Children have already opened their bundles, spreading blankets out on the floor and wrapping themselves up in them. The Old People also lug their stuff in, pitch camp under the table.*]

K [*to the Husband*]: You should have gone to the director's place: there's more room there . . .

The Husband: But we wouldn't be let in there.

Mrs. Grubach: You can't stay here!

[*Outside in the hall Miss Bürstner and the Captain appear.*]

Captain: What disgraceful behavior!

Miss Bürstner: Is that his family?

[*The Woman closes the door from inside. The Husband unpacks pots, sets them on the table. The Woman empties a sack of cloths onto the floor. The chairs are rearranged, the objects on the floor shoved aside. K sinks back onto the bed. Darkness.*]

ACT THREE

Scene 21

[A meeting. The effect of large dimensions. At the head of the table with the mirrored surface: the Public Prosecutor. To his left: an empty chair for the General, then the Captain, then Miss Bürstner. To his right: the Director, Rabensteiner, Kaminer, Leni. At the foot of the table: K.]

Kaminer [holding forth at the table]: As I was saying—the takeover of the factories went off to the satisfaction of the ministry. As adjutant to the general, Captain Lanz can give you . . .

Captain: The general sees great possibilities for development!

Kaminer: And the main thing is: we're playing now in the world market!

Director [this time without his smile]: He will come, won't he?

Captain: He's definitely coming!

Kaminer: On my visit to New York I was struck by the extraordinary co-operation displayed . . .

Director [to K]: Why didn't you undertake the trip yourself?

Captain: We know why—family matters!

Rabensteiner: Mr. Kaminer had prepared everything. He was expected at the branch office . . .

Director [to K]: Did the presentation not seem to you quite ready? Did you want further information?

K: I . . .

Captain: But he was occupied with his family! [Laughs.] . . . It's a singing group. They always sing at night!

Kaminer: That must be very disruptive. Do you allow it to go on?

Miss Bürstner: I for one can't stand it any more.

Director: You still owe us an explanation of the reason for the delay. We've been waiting all winter. The situation was ripe. We almost lost the

Scene 21: *Left to right:* **Director, Rabensteiner, Kaminer, Public Prosecutor, Leni, K, Captain, Miss Bürstner**

deal. If we hadn't sent Mr. Kaminer—who has now in effect taken over many of your duties . . .

K: Sir, I'm working on it. So many uncertainties have arisen. If Mr. Kaminer thinks he's in a position to solve all problems, then of course I'm ready to resign . . .

Public Prosecutor: Certainly not, Josef! You must remain at your post. You see, it's precisely your thoroughness that we value in you. To be sure, you're a bit slow. Sometimes you have too many reservations when one really should decide quickly. But we have plenty of other people who can jump right into things. You must just evaluate everything. Then we benefit from the results.

Director: All the same! You had already made the contacts. The American ambassador spoke enthusiastically of your proposals . . .

Public Prosecutor: I assume, Josef, that you took every detail into consideration . . . not least all the ideological and ethical issues . . .

K: I've proceeded with these perspectives in mind . . .

Miss Bürstner: But the affairs of the bank—he doesn't take them into account.

K: Documents are being withheld from me.

Rabensteiner: That may have to do with the new arrangements we're putting in place.

Kaminer: It's a matter of protecting the workplace. Of strict secrecy in selecting and installing the teams.

Director: But no new hiring!

Kaminer: Except for the new industries!

Director: Downsizing is necessary there too. As you know, growth must never be visible on the outside. Expansion through economizing. Constantly stress one's hard-pressed situation.

Kaminer: We make transfers primarily from the transport sector. That's where our most reliable people are.

Captain: Not enough attention is paid to the resources available to us in the military. Soldiers have learned to act in a brave and disciplined way. Bravery, I say, is a quality that needs to be properly appreciated again!

Public Prosecutor: Mr. Lanz, I don't underestimate your officers. But don't forget that the fusion of the economic and the military spheres calls for redoubled security measures. Only the best must be deployed in each area. Exchange of experiences—yes! Cooperation—yes! But vigilance is necessary on every front. And at the same time the *entirety* of the project must be kept in view!

Captain: Yes sir, Mr. General Director!

Public Prosecutor: And Josef, what is the problem with the bank?

K: I can't quite see it. There seems to be some forgery going on there . . .

Public Prosecutor [*to Miss Bürstner*]: Sit down together with Josef. Investigate where the mistakes are hidden. Josef—he has a nose for that. I want order to prevail in my house. Clarity and honesty.

[*The General enters. He wears a uniform with decorations. All rise. The Public Prosecutor shows the General to his chair. All take their places. Slowly the stage goes dark.*]

Scene 22

[*The room in the boardinghouse. The lamp burns above the oval table. The rest of the room is in very subdued lighting. The bed is unmade. The statuettes are shoved into a corner, half concealed by crumpled newspapers. Many of the pictures are missing from the walls. The vent is still plastered over. The door of the clothes closet hangs open. It is filled with things in disarray. A few drawers in*

the chest are pulled out. They too are full of cloths and towels. Pieces of cloth-
ing lie on the washstand, dirty laundry is in the sink. Laundered rags hang on
a clothesline drawn across the center of the room. Shoes and clothes lie scattered
about. The Children are sleeping on the floor under a blanket. The Old People are
sitting under the table between bundles. The Woman is stirring a pot that she has
placed on a pile of books. The Husband sits on a chair, his legs spread out in front
of him, and snores from time to time. K stands waiting at the open door in the
background.

    Miss Bürstner stands by the table. K offers her a chair, pushes aside plates
and dishes containing the remains of food.

    Miss Bürstner sits down reluctantly. K sits down beside her, grasps her hands,
which she immediately withdraws.]

K: Now we're here. Now we can really talk with each other.

Miss Bürstner: But we can't talk here.

K: We're not alone in your room either . . .

Miss Bürstner: There's only my confidante there . . .

K: These people here are also very close to me. Here we can say every-
    thing . . .

Miss Bürstner: How can you expect Mrs. Grubach to accommodate all
    these people?

K: I pay the rent for all of them.

Miss Bürstner: What do they actually do?

K: They are honorable people. They conduct a business.

Miss Bürstner: What kind?

K: They collect rags. Wash the rags. Sell them as dustrags or cleaning
    cloths.

Miss Bürstner: And you imagine I would confide my secrets to you in this
    place . . .

K: Then let me begin. Miss Bürstner, we live separated only by a wall. I
    hear each of your steps just as you hear mine. I hear the rustle of your
    clothes, I hear when you lie down. My consciousness is filled by your
    existence. Merely being in this house, your presence fills me up. How
    much more strongly I feel you in the place where we spend the day
    together. There we're no longer protected but bear a responsibility for
    something that's become immensely important to us both. If we're
    close neighbors when we're here, there we're completely bound to each
    other. Here a whisper is already like a provocation, but there . . . in

that palace . . . you compel me to an involvement that's like an inner upheaval . . .

Miss Bürstner: I don't compel you to anything . . .

K: When something defines my life to such a degree, it must have a point of origin . . .

Miss Bürstner: It can come from myriad different directions . . .

K: It comes from you alone. I'm constantly wondering: what's your hand doing now . . . in what direction is it pointing . . .

Miss Bürstner: That has nothing—nothing—to do with you.

K: And your mouth: what words is it forming now, what orders is it giving, what truth is it speaking, what lies . . .

Miss Bürstner: I never lie!

K: You lie incessantly! I keep trying, till I'm almost in despair, to hear something true from you. Miss Bürstner, we're both caught up in something that's basically hostile to us, that wants to destroy us, and for which we're nevertheless working tirelessly, as if we wanted to race even faster to our ruin . . .

Miss Bürstner [bursting into laughter]: Do you want to rescue me?

K: We've arrived at such a close relationship with each other, how are we to stand it, knowing so much about each other . . . we can only manage if we extend our knowledge still further, to where we belong together, are bound together, so that you and I, yes, you and I consti- tute a doubly strong force . . . for that's the only way we can blast our way out . . . together . . .

Miss Bürstner [laughing more shrilly]: Listen! He wants to rescue me! Listen, you rabble, he wants to rescue me! He, who owns nothing but useless junk, he's promising me a better world! [Piercing laughter. A heavy knock on the wall from behind.] Yes, my sweet! Come! Help me! [She throws herself off the chair, writhes on the floor.] He's assaulting me! He's attacking me! He's trying to rape me! [The door in the background is yanked open. Miss Montag paddles in. The Captain follows her. The family displays no involvement whatever.]

Miss Montag: What's happened, dearest—

Captain: He isn't able to harm you!

[They kneel down beside Miss Bürstner, lift her up.]

Miss Bürstner [convulsed by laughing]: He wanted bank secrets from me! He wanted to force me! Like this! [She puts her hands in a choke hold around her neck.] He wanted to strangle me! [*The Captain and Miss Montag stand up, carrying Miss Bürstner between them. Miss Bürstner's laughter has turned into sobbing.*]

Captain: A box of insecticide, and then lock the door . . . that's what's needed here . . .

[*They carry Miss Bürstner out. The door falls shut. K sits motionless at the table. The two Old People begin to hum quietly to themselves. It's not really a song, rather a monotonous, rhythmic groaning. The Woman and her Husband join in. But not until the voices of the Children are added in does something like a chorus, a liturgy take shape. The stage slowly goes dark.*]

Scene 23

[*In the office. Only the desk is illuminated. K is in the chair. Leni, her legs drawn up, sits on the desktop.*]

K: To me also art seemed for a long time to be the one genuine . . . happiness . . .

Leni: You hesitate?

K: The word happiness . . .

Leni: It cannot exist.

K: Since when, actually?

Leni: Since you've been able to think.

K: But I've thought about it constantly . . .

Leni: And promptly rejected it every time.

K: Why?

Leni: You say it yourself.

K: Because . . . because it always had to turn into a lie . . .

Leni: Who makes it into a lie?

K: Did I make it into a lie? No. It should have been a truth. It was a possibility, after all. Otherwise I wouldn't have thought about it all the time. Sometimes, perhaps only when I'm asleep, it's there. Then comes the awakening . . .

Leni: And when you're awake and think about it?

K: Then I must be like the painter. He has to weep when his thoughts touch it.

Leni: But why weep—about happiness?

K: Don't say the word again!

Leni: Happiness.

K: Be quiet!

Leni: What is there about it that you can't tolerate?

K: That it just hangs there like a foreign body, reminding us only of our
degradation . . .

Leni: The painter said something different.

K: He said . . . it opened a way toward freedom . . .

Leni: And what did he mean by freedom?

K: Forgetting. He meant, forget everything that I'm unable to forget . . .

Leni: He didn't mean that. He meant: accept everything. Reject nothing.

K: That's impossible! How can he see the horror around us and still find
peace? How can art fulfill him when the horror all around is growing?

Leni: It lightens the burden.

K: How can it lighten anything—when everything is only becoming
heavier . . .

Leni: For the moment perhaps. Isn't that enough?

K: No! Relief can only truly exist when you know it'll endure . . .

Leni: Isn't it enough to sense that possibility?

K: That would just be deception . . .

Leni: Why would it be deception?

K: Because it can only be an escape. And that would contradict the resolve
to expose oneself to everything . . .

Leni: Oh, that's no contradiction. It's no contradiction to make a sign
pointing to the suffering that would tear you apart. It's no contradiction to make eternal what will disappear in an instant. It's no contradiction to love what destroys you.

K: Leni . . . what am I to do?

Leni: You should give yourself completely to your terrible love, even if it
destroys you . . .

[Darkness.]

Scene 24

[The meeting room in the shed. The podium is now diagonally across stage front.
Miss Montag is at the high desk, half turned toward the background. In the semi-
darkness the audience is barely visible. Among those standing around the podium
at front are Kaminer, Rabensteiner, Willem, and Franz. At the outset they too
are not yet recognizable. Leni and K are to one side. The scene opens with a wave
of shouts, whistles, laughter.]

Miss Montag [*speaking into the microphone*]: So I gave him a proper earful. And how did I get him to talk? Well, first I tore my clothes open in front of him.

Voice (Kaminer): You with your crooked bones!

Miss Montag: Yes, I showed him that everything about me is crooked and bent!

Voice: Do you have breasts?

Miss Montag: Nonsense! All you can see there are ribs. So: he had this little pile of misery in front of him. And I used my wretchedness to make him soft. In me you see all the humiliated ones, I said to him. In me you see all who suffer adversity. I speak for all defiled bodies. Look, I said, at the traces of torture on my body. In front of him I made myself into the woman who gives birth to dead children, or whose children, if they survive, soon croak from hunger and disease, or, if they still survive that, die in the massacres . . . [*Whistling, yelling.*]

Miss Montag: What's the matter? Don't you belong among those people? . . . No answer. Now you've lost your voice, just like he did. Normally he talks like a book, but then he just sat there like a dummy. With you all it's different. You've never learned how to express yourselves. Or it's been beaten out of you.

Voice (Willem): You dirty cow!

Miss Montag: Finally, someone capable of saying something. The other guy didn't even say that much. I grabbed him by his tie and asked him what he was moaning about . . .

Voice (Franz): Why him exactly? He's been finished for a long time!

Miss Montag: Oh no! He's quite senior. From people like him you hear a very special kind of music. What do you call it—compassion!

Voice (Rabensteiner): Compassion is an excellent quality!

Miss Montag: It is, isn't it? They persuade you that they have only good things in mind. And they do. But the good is only for themselves. The one I'm talking about is one of the leading reformer types. And so, I began by setting out for him the full dimensions of the suffering. And sure enough, tears came to his eyes. And then he began to express beliefs. Yes, these reformers are always great ones for expressing themselves. They express their solidarity with the weak. They say they've always been on the side of the weak. Yes, someone used to spit in their soup when they were children. They were weak then. With their sympathy for the weak they make themselves important. They grow big with their sympathy. Suddenly they're carrying the whole world on their shoulder. They take hold of an entire continent. Things must get better here, they cry. And things do get better. For them! Always for them!

Voice (Willem): What's she talking about? Can't someone shut her up?

Miss Montag: Ah yes—shut me up! There was once a man who wanted to make a woman shut up. He knelt down before her and gawked at her with blurry eyes. The first thing he said was, there's such power flowing from you, it must be directed at me since I feel it so strongly. But then he said she couldn't do anything herself with this power. Because she came from poverty. Had lived as a child in the slum areas. Where he himself would never go. And now he wanted to rescue her. To rescue her with her power. I'll make your power my own, he cried. Give me your power! Bestow your power upon me! And what does he call that? . . . Love! [Laughter, whistles.] You all doubt this love? Perhaps it really is love—for him! He talks about her strength. But really he wants to rob her of her strength. Wants to see her become weak! Yes—he can only love someone even weaker than himself. He throws himself before her, in order to use her to build himself up and then to push her down into the dirt. [Franz has clambered onto the podium. Sneaks up on Miss Montag.] And because none of this works for him, he turns to someone who he knows is stronger and will remain so. He can't get at her with love. Not with his kind of love. He begs her to tell him what to do . . .

[Before Franz reaches her, she has nimbly leaped from the podium. Tumult breaks out.]

Willem: Don't let her get away!

[Scuffles. The dissolution of the meeting goes in two directions. One breaks out toward the side, with waves and whirlings. Miss Montag flees in this direction together with Miss Bürstner, who has suddenly appeared beside her. The other wave tries to move in the opposite direction. In this confusion, which seems, however, to become orderly again, are to be seen Kaminer, Willem, and Franz. Leni draws K along with her. As the stage goes dark, the noise continues.]

Scene 25

[A sharp vertical ray of light illuminates a section of the crowd again. The movements are now weaker. Murmuring, shuffling of steps. At the front, vividly lit, the Public Prosecutor, the Director, the General, the Captain, the American Ambassador. They are joined by Rabensteiner, Kaminer, Willem, and Franz. Finally, Leni and K. In the background an obscure to and fro of groups in motion.]

Director [calling to the rear]: And so the new public reception building has been opened. May it serve the people's peaceful life together, as well as justice and freedom!

[Applause. The Director sees K, goes up to him, leads him to the American Ambassador.]

Director [with his smile]: Your Excellency, I'd like to introduce you to the person responsible . . .

Ambassador: [shaking K's hand]: An audacious and challenging action! And yet one that harmonizes with our aspirations.

K: It wasn't I . . . the painter . . . [Looks around, searching. Willem and Franz bring Titorelli forward from the rear. The painter is wearing his gray overalls. Walks somewhat unsteadily, appears to be drunk.]

Ambassador [to Titorelli]: Truly extraordinary, the pictures you've painted for us.

Titorelli: Not for you—against you . . . [turns away.]

Director: But since they're now hanging on our walls, they give expression to our essence!

Titorelli [murmuring]: Ah yes . . . your essence . . .

Ambassador: I'm still feeling . . . how do you say it . . . deeply stirred, shaken!

[The painter moves off, supported by Willem and Franz.]

Director: Yes . . . I too was in doubt for a time, wasn't sure whether we could dare to present this problematic, dissonant world . . .

Ambassador: Which, however, completely corresponds to the world we live in! That's the point: this genuineness, this . . . nakedness . . . mirrors the forces that threaten us . . .

Director: Forces which, as we show with our purchasing, we understand how to exorcise and control!

General: I just hope there's no real explosive there! Some of those things look to me as though they might blow up any minute!

Ambassador: That's just what's thrilling about them! Rarely in modern art have form and content been fused into such unity!

Director [smiling]: I'm delighted, Your Excellency, that you, as the representative of the most powerful industrial nation, are so well disposed toward our efforts . . .

Ambassador [patting K on the shoulder]: I wish we had experts like you!

Director [to K]: Yes, my friend, I'd like to say you've really reached the heights!

Kaminer [stepping forward]: We hear he even did some of the painting! One picture in particular: the one with the prisoners in chains and one of them sitting by the stake about to be garrotted — he's said to have painted that one himself . . .

Director: What are you saying? Which picture? I didn't see that one at all! [Turns to K.] Is that right? Did you paint it?

K: No, I did nothing! Nothing!

Director [looking around]: Titorelli! Titorelli!
[Willem and Franz push the painter forward as he sways from side to side.]

Director: Mr. Titorelli, is it true that others help you with the painting?

Titorelli [mumbling]: Oh yes, everyone helps me . . . whole armies work on every picture . . .

Director [pointing to K]: This man too?

Titorelli: Yes, he too. And you. And the American over there. And the general. [He loses his balance, tries to hold on, and grabs the Captain.] . . . And this one too. He was at my place. Wanted to paint everything alone. [Sees the Public Prosecutor.] And that one especially! You can't even show what he painted!
[Willem and Franz are about to drag the painter away. The Director restrains them.]

Director: So where is that picture, the one with the prisoners?

Titorelli: What prisoners?

Kaminer: One of them is about to be executed . . .

Titorelli: What do you mean?

Kaminer: He's sitting in chains . . . by a stake . . .

Titorelli [laughing]: Oh, that one! The worker! He's working on the roads. He's sitting on a rock. I don't know anymore if he's holding his breakfast roll or his pay packet!

[Everyone laughs. Willem and Franz shove the painter away. The Director draws the Ambassador and the General into a group. The Public Prosecutor, his arm around K, joins them. They move forward a few steps. Rabensteiner, Kaminer, and the Captain join them. Leni withdraws into the background while the group moves farther forward.]

General: He mentioned armies . . . armies . . . what did he mean by that . . . [Darkness.]

Scene 26

[The group approaches the conference table. They take their places. At the top: the Public Prosecutor. To his left: the American Ambassador, the Director, the Captain, an empty chair for Miss Bürstner. To his right: the General, Rabensteiner, Kaminer, Leni. At the bottom: K.]

Public Prosecutor [to K]: Josef, what can there be in the world that's more than this?

K: Live now in accordance . . .

Ambassador: I understand! Integrate art and reality. You know, I'm really an artist too. I've always understood my professional activity as artistic work!

Director: Yes, we must think creatively if we are to take on the great questions, questions that concern whole continents . . .

Ambassador: And the more responsibility we have, the more important it is to emphasize that respect for humanity is the trademark of our endeavors!

Captain: Especially now, with increasing unrest everywhere!

Kaminer: When daily we must strengthen the public image of our alternative way!

Ambassador: Just as the director in his speech emphasized our ideals!

General: They simply cannot be invoked often enough! And by us! For the enemy is using them also. We must present them even more convincingly, so that it becomes clear that truth is on our side.

Ambassador: That's right, General! Yet we must admit that we, even though we are, as they say, in the driver's seat, occasionally feel ourselves to be helpless.

General: Not the slightest doubt must be permitted to arise that we are the ones who guarantee peace!

Ambassador: As an artistic person who's been thrown into politics, I must repeat that behind us there are other powers capable of snatching away from us all the plans and programs we produce; I mean powers against which we are helpless, that perhaps reside within ourselves . . .

Director: Is it not precisely this humanistic principle, this capacity for self-criticism, for questioning everything that's been achieved, this spiritual freedom—that makes you, and of course us, your allies, so superior? For I too, who now [*suddenly smiling*] will assume the office of economics minister, I know that existential uncertainty of which you speak. To live with this uncertainty, constantly to overcome it, and to give political meaning to this overcoming—that is where I see our strength!

Public Prosecutor [*to the Ambassador*]: Your Excellency, it is truly admirable that, as we contemplate a new era of expansion, you should remind us of our human weaknesses!

Ambassador: Gentlemen, I cannot see the future as other than the way your painter, in the frieze of pictures . . .

Director: Just as I said—nothing good will come from these pictures!

Ambassador: As people who think and shape the world around them, however, we must start from this premise. The division is a reality not only with us and with you. We find it throughout the world. On the one hand there are the enlightened ones, ourselves, whose knowledge is highly developed, and on the other hand there are, how do you call them, those who live in want . . .

Public Prosecutor [*to K*]: Josef—surely the ambassador's words come from the depths of *your* heart!

Ambassador: In that other zone there is depression, gathering disaster . . .

Rabensteiner: Which is to be prevented!

Ambassador: While with us there is this monstrous, seemingly unshakable order, that still gives us security but that also—since we have an inkling of the catastrophe lurking behind it—makes us sad . . .

General: And all that serves to strengthen us in our ethics, our morality!

Ambassador: Alas, we are prisoners of our philosophy! For all the wisdom we impart to the world, our hands remain tied. We cannot, on our own initiative, found the empire of peace and freedom, however much we would like to do so. Let me say it clearly—we must work against ourselves. And we must do so by enabling the world to see through us, to confront us with our errors and falsehoods . . .

Public Prosecutor [*laughing*]: Your Excellency, you've expressed yourself in an exemplary democratic manner!

Ambassador [*leans forward, buries his face for a second in his hands*]: If it's not already too late!

Director: For us it is a new beginning!

[*Miss Bürstner has appeared. Radiant, elegant. The men rise briefly as she takes the empty seat on the left side of the table. After her silent greeting she nods to K in an especially friendly way.*]

Public Prosecutor [*pointing to K*]: And, Your Excellency, we have assigned the office of director to someone in tune with yourself in his sensibility and elevated convictions . . . [*Darkness.*]

Scene 27

[*A large space, the dimensions of which cannot be seen in the semi-darkness. Only Leni and K, sitting on the floor, are illuminated.*]

Leni: You ask why, so I'll tell you. It's because they still need you. The instant you're no longer needed, you'll be dropped.

K: How can they need me and even promote me, when I no longer do anything for them . . .

Leni: Oh, you've done enough that still has to run its course. Until that happens it's a plus that you're still there.

K: Since spring I've been spending my time in the central office doing nothing but sitting. I haven't dictated a single memorandum. I don't even draft reports.

Leni: Meanwhile, most of what you actually did put into practice has been taken into the propaganda division. In the glossy American pamphlets, in the brochures for South Africa, there you loom large. Your remarks have been translated into all the world languages.

K: I know nothing about that . . .

Leni: You're not supposed to know anything about it. You wondered why you, as director, have been deprived of freedom of movement. They say they want to save you the trouble, so that you can concentrate totally on the new tasks. Yes, you're free to look around everywhere, just not in the propaganda division.

K: I didn't know it was above me in the hierarchy.

Leni: It's a big new area.

K: I asked the public prosecutor recently whether propaganda wasn't really in my sphere of responsibility. He just dismissed the question . . .

Leni: If you went there, you'd recognize nothing of what's been done with your ideas.

K: Leni, I can hardly understand any more how I could spend years in this enterprise . . .

Leni: That's why they kept you on. Because you don't understand who benefits from all your efforts.

K: To me that was right and proper . . .

Leni: Yes, you supported what was right. You embodied fair play. You were morally unimpeachable. And you were able to give expression to this attitude.

K: Why do you say that? It was the very basis of the institution. I wouldn't have been there otherwise . . .

Leni: And you wouldn't otherwise have advanced beyond the insurance division.

K: But it was there that they reproached me for my weaknesses . . .

Leni: In order to get even more out of you.

K: What did they get?

Leni: You still don't know?

K: Perhaps . . . no . . .

Leni: The firm needed someone in the leadership who was above suspicion, whose honor could be invoked in all negotiations, all new ventures. You have only to be named and the whole undertaking is truth itself.

K: Even if I no longer believe I can do anything more . . .

Leni: Your innocence was well suited to everything that was undertaken . . . without your knowledge.

K: An insignificant person like me . . .

Leni: Such an insignificant person can give a face to power.

K: Without having an effect on it?

Leni: Without having an effect on it.

K: How can you say that to me . . .

Leni: I can say it now.

K: Why . . . now . . .

Leni: I've been dismissed.

[Darkness.]

Scene 28

[A meeting. The space around the table with the mirrored surface is dark. The table is seen head on. In the center: the Public Prosecutor. To his left: the American Ambassador, the Director (now a Minister, with hair turned white), the Captain, and Miss Bürstner. To his right: the General, Rabensteiner, and Kaminer. In front, facing them: K.]

Ambassador: Nevertheless I wouldn't say that war must come!

General: That's why the warnings must be strengthened! People have lived in peace for too long. That has a demoralizing effect. They say, who would gain from a war. The dangerousness of the enemy must be made clear.

Kaminer: But some journalists are leaving us in the lurch.

Captain: We've been too gentle with them.

Ambassador: Never forget that our strength is based on tolerance . . . There must not even be the appearance of suppressing freedom of speech. Rather we must demand absolute freedom of the press. Where are the suggestions of our director on this?

K: Your Excellency, there's more and more evidence of a sense of impotence . . . it's as if people wanted to hide themselves away . . . only rarely do you still find individual expressions of opinion . . .

Director/Minister [recognizable by his special smile]: Perhaps we've gone too far with our threats. I'm wondering, don't people believe us about the crisis any more? True, people accepted pay cuts and downsizing—in order to save other jobs. But the lights are still on. The trains run. There's still enough to buy. People aren't convinced by the losses so far. And ultimately we must have the cooperation of the majority, in order to maintain our system.

Rabensteiner: I would still like to say that the planning indications of our new director were of great value. He's the one who recognized the exhaustion, the decay of the opposition. We hardly needed to intervene. The feuds and slanders were carried out by the opposition's people themselves.

Kaminer: All we did was intensify the atmosphere of uncertainty just a

Scene 28: *Left to right:* A functionary, Kaminer, Rabensteiner, General, Public Prosecutor, American Ambassador, Director, Captain, Miss Bürstner. K in front.

little—and faster than we could hope, these vacillators, these eternal weaklings came over to our side. Aren't many of their leaders with us today who were reviling us just a few years ago?

Ambassador: Our tactics were correct. For a while we allowed some latitude to the movements of—how shall I call them—of the wretched ones. We even granted them a few small successes and victories. And thus the attention of the most restless of their supporters was diverted—away from domestic issues toward a distant revolutionary goal. And when the heroic idea ceased to be attractive, when these people had to face both everyday desperation and the unpleasantness of organizational matters, then the supporters' attention was quickly lost—as always, when there are no weapons . . .

Public Prosecutor: For our sphere this means that the emotional excesses of youth—of the impoverished—are useful from time to time. A residual urge to do something fizzles out, and then it suffices, as our director aptly remarked, to pick out a few in order to exemplify through them the general hopelessness of resistance.

Director/Minister [*with his smile*]: And how is the arming of our people going?

Kaminer: We've continued the equipping of the workforce. The training is of the athletic variety. Only a small proportion have real guard duty. Most are in the welfare office, the communication system, housing agency . . .

Ambassador [*waves him away*]: Not so much detail!

Kaminer: They don't arouse the slightest suspicion at work.

Ambassador [*disgusted*]: Stop talking about that junk. Our task here is to concern ourselves with great strategies. The goal is to replace the antiquated concept of equality with a new—legalized—conception. What suggestions does our director have for that?

[*K is silent.*]

Miss Bürstner: Up till now we've worked with what we still possessed of the director's instructions. Unfortunately, they've recently become rather sparse. I say unfortunately, because I'm worried about him. [*She turns to the Public Prosecutor.*] . . . Mr. General Director, perhaps it would be possible for me to win him back again completely for our team.

Director/Minister: Are the problems that existed between you cleared away?

Miss Bürstner: Oh, there's now absolute clarity in the bank's affairs!

Rabensteiner: It had been delayed because a central security system was being installed in the bank . . .

Kaminer: Because the people entrusted with the security had to be especially reliable . . .

Public Prosecutor (*turning to Miss Bürstner*): Then, my dear, give it a try! Take him with you right away. Let's lose no time, talk things through with him . . .

[*Miss Bürstner has risen. She takes K by the hand, leads him out. Darkness.*]

Scene 29

[*Miss Bürstner's office. Similar to K's office. On the desk are Willem and Franz, naked except for Japanese loincloths, locked in a wrestlers' embrace. Enter Miss Bürstner, drawing K along after her. She chases away the two men with yells and blows, drives them, by kicking them, toward the closet in the background: its door is open. Willem and Franz disappear into it. Miss Bürstner kicks the door shut. She immediately tears off her own dress, draws K to the desk, and seats herself on top of it.*]

Miss Bürstner: Yes . . . now I'm ready for you! Yes! We're like each other! Of course you were the boy with clean stockings while I went bare-foot, dressed in a sack—but in the extent of our humiliation we're no different from each other! You wanted to have me down in the dirt—now you can have me among the bank safes! For that's how it had to be, my little one—I had to rise in order to be a match for you, you had to fall in order to do me justice . . . now we can unite, for the misery we endured was the same for both of us!

K [*drawing back*]: No, that's not how I wanted it! Not here!

Miss Bürstner: Not here . . . in the bank! But not in your place either, among all your garbage!

K: We must look for a third . . .

Miss Bürstner: There is no third possibility! There isn't! It must be here! You said it yourself, we've sneaked into this institution, we've conquered something jointly—here we can become strong . . . powerful . . .

K: We must leave! Leave this place!

Miss Bürstner: We can't leave! We can't get any further! Only here can we overcome everything that stands in our way . . .

K: Here it's worst of all! With corpses in the closet! With shooting on the street! Listen how they scream, how they run . . . then fall . . .

Miss Bürstner: Nothing! I hear nothing! It's completely quiet. We have guards. We have iron doors. There is peace here. Come!

K [*withdraws further*]: No—here we are prisoners!

Miss Bürstner: Only here, only here are we safe!

K: To stay here means our death!

Miss Bürstner: But that's peace—the very peace you were looking for!

[*She breaks into her piercing laughter. K flees. At that moment the Captain and the Public Prosecutor enter from the opposite side. They grab Miss Bürstner, pull her off the desk, drag her out. Her laughter has turned into shrill sobbing. Darkness.*]

Scene 30

[*The room in the boardinghouse. K hurries in from the side as the door in the background is flung open and Willem and Franz rush in. They are in work clothes, carrying a ladder. They chase the family out of their piles of rags and drive them together into a corner. Whoever then stirs is beaten or shoved. Franz and Willem place the ladder against the wall underneath the glued-on piece of cardboard. Out-*]

side in the hall a guard (theatrical extra) is visible. Franz climbs up and tears off the piece of cardboard. Immediately a violent rush of air comes from the vent. The scraps of cardboard flutter in the draft.

K stands in the middle of the room. Outside in the hall Mrs. Grubach can be seen. She claps her hands together over her face. Miss Montag shows up too, lugging suitcases and bundles.]

Willem [to Mrs. Grubach]: Don't get excited, Mrs. Grubach! You know you're getting something much better!

Franz: You're admitted to the beautiful old folks' home. Your own room — a privilege for the company's most deserving employees!

Willem [to K]: And finally you're free from all these beggars and thieves!

Franz: Yes, this ruin has to go. A new district will be built here! Airy and bright! That's our motto!

Willem: Whoever doesn't want to understand that will be taught it. [Willem and Franz convey the family out of the room. Each person, as he or she is pushed out, is grabbed by the guard and shoved further. The Old Woman falls down, the Children cling to her. They are yanked up again. The Husband shows resistance, is beaten down, and crawls out on all fours. Mrs. Grubach has entered the room, her hands tensely gripping her apron.]

Mrs. Grubach: Oh Josef, Josef, my son! How could that happen to us!

K: Let it be, mother, let it be . . .

[Darkness.]

Scene 31

[A stroll. Dusk. The Public Prosecutor, the Director/Minister, the American Ambassador, the General, the Captain, Rabensteiner, and Kaminer. In the dim light the Public Prosecutor, Ambassador, and General appear white-haired, and the others seem to have grown gray.]

Director/Minister: Today we stand more modest, more upstanding, more respected than a year ago. We too are blooming like the spring and approaching our summer . . .

Captain [breathes deeply]: Oh, this air!

Director/Minister [to the Ambassador]: For the ceaseless confrontation between ourselves — the advanced societies — and the primitives has become such an everyday phenomenon that it no longer surprises anyone . . .

Kaminer: The collision comes, the revolt flares up, burns a few moments, is crushed, is close to suffocation—and if it doesn't want to expire, it begs us for help . . .

Ambassador: Yes, givers and receivers. Isn't that the new equality? What we take in raw materials, we give back in education and technology. Whoever refuses to grasp that . . . is taught a lesson. Nothing is so useful as the school of hunger.

Rabensteiner: What a sense of responsibility!

Captain: And what patience, Your Excellency!

Ambassador: You practice it yourself, Colonel!

Public Prosecutor: Ah—this quality of patience! It has become part of our flesh and blood. What would we be without this patience . . .

Ambassador: Which keeps us young!

Director/Minister [*smiling fiercely*]: Which gives us this superiority! While others think they have to fight . . . we barely exert ourselves. We expand . . . as if following a natural law!

Rabensteiner: By means of endurance and . . . kindness!

General, Captain, Kaminer: Kindness!

Rabensteiner: We can always wait . . . while if *they* wait, they go to pieces! We close down industries, drive monopolies to bankruptcy!

General, Captain, Kaminer: Enduring! Kindly!

Rabensteiner: And not—this must be stressed—not in order to enrich ourselves . . . oh no! [*Laughs.*]

Ambassador [*chimes in with the laughter*]: No, we can hardly become any richer!

Rabensteiner: Our profit hasn't been the issue for a long time. The issue is rather . . . to destroy the profits of others . . .

Ambassador: And thus we destroy the destructiveness that grows out of opposition to us!

General, Captain, Kaminer: Love of peace!

Public Prosecutor: That's why our hardness is generosity. That's why we show the enemy no mercy! But we must become still stronger! What it costs us—we barely notice it. But the enemy will surely disintegrate because of the arms buildup we impose on him . . .

General: And the best means that remains at our disposal for the resolution of all conflicts is . . .

Everyone [*except the General*]: War!

Scene 33: K, Franz, Willem

Ambassador: Then we can move finally to the realization of our educational mission!

Everyone [*except the Ambassador*]: As the true force for peace!

Public Prosecutor: What a shame—that Josef isn't with us anymore . . .

[*The group leaves.*]

Scene 32

[*A crowd rushes past in the opposite direction, fleeing chaotically.*]

Voice: Quick! They're coming!

Voice: The wounded! We've got to fetch them!

Voice: No, keep going! Don't stop!

[*The crowd disappears. Leni and K enter from the side, stand on the empty stage.*]

K: Where to now?

Leni: Stay hidden. Let no one see you. Go now. Don't look back at me. Come to the painter's place tomorrow before dawn. I'll prepare our escape.

K: Tomorrow . . .

Leni: Yes, tomorrow, on your birthday . . .

[*Leni leaves. K remains standing, irresolute.*]

Scene 33

[Shots are heard in the distance. The crowd rushes back past. A few wounded are hauled along. One of those running, the speaker of the Fifth Voice, calls out to K.]

Fifth Voice: Don't hang around here, man!

[The shots are now closer. K suddenly doubles up. The crowd disappears. K falls down sideways. Lies there, doubled up, his legs drawn up under him. Willem and Franz appear, in leather uniforms. They stroll up to K. Franz prods him with his foot. Willem bends over him, shakes his head. They turn away from him, and move on.]

Willem: Like a dog . . .

[Franz and Willem leave. After a few moments Leni hurries in. She kneels down behind K. Touches his face. Suddenly stiffens. Then she thrusts her clenched fists into the air. Utters a terrible cry. Darkness.]

THE KAFKA CONNECTION

While the story of *The New Trial* is in no way dependent on Kafka's novel, Weiss has inserted explicit references to Kafka all the way through: the characters' names, of course, and parallel images reminding us that Kafka's bureaucratic scenario is being translated into the framework of a more consciously global capitalism. This appendix lists the most striking of these overt references. The page numbers for Kafka refer to the new translation of *The Trial* by Breon Mitchell (New York: Random House, 1999). Permission to quote is gratefully acknowledged.

Scene 1
While the frame of Kafka's famous opening arrest scene is clearly recalled (K in bed, guards named Franz and Willem), direct verbal allusions are conspicuous by their absence.

Scene 2
Mrs. Grubach: "After all, it's his birthday."
As in Kafka (pp. 6, 225), the events of *The New Trial* span precisely one year, between the protagonist's thirtieth and thirty-first birthdays.

Scene 3
Mrs. Grubach: "But don't take it so much to heart." Mrs. Grubach, in Kafka: ". . . but above all you mustn't take it too seriously" (p. 22). "Don't take it so hard" (p. 24).

Scene 4
The objects on K's desk and their order and disorder play a thematic role in

The New Trial. In Kafka, a comparable significance is initially assigned to objects in Miss Bürstner's room: the inspector is "arranging with both hands the few objects lying on the nightstand – a candle with matches, a book, and a pin-cushion – as if they were tools he required for the hearing" (p. 13). And in the evening Miss Bürstner notices "my photos have been all mixed up. That's really annoying" (p. 28). Much later we see K in his office: "But instead of working he swung about in his chair, moved a few items around slowly on his desk, and then, without being aware of it, left his arm outstretched on the desktop and remained sitting motionless with bowed head" (p. 111).

Scene 8

A complex friendship between K and Public Prosecutor Hasterer is evoked at length in a chapter Kafka never completed: "if K's right to sit (at the courtroom table) was ever questioned, he was fully justified in calling Hasterer for support. K thus achieved a particularly privileged position, for Hasterer was as respected as he was feared . . . K had the impression that if Hasterer couldn't convince his opponent, he at least frightened him, for many drew back when he merely raised his outstretched finger" (p. 246).

The telephone, prominent in Kafka's novel, plays a role only in this scene. In Kafka, K himself "improvised" the conditions of the Sunday appointment with the court: "some sort of stubbornness had prevented K from taking a cab; he had an aversion to even the slightest outside help in this affair of his . . . He was now running to get there by nine if at all possible, although he had not even been given a specific hour at which to appear" (p. 38).

Scene 9

Miss Montag's movements, stressed by Weiss, are briefly mentioned by Kafka, again in an unfinished chapter: "A French teacher, a German by the name of Montag, a weak, pale young woman with a slight limp who had been living in a room of her own till then, was moving in with Fräulein Bürstner. For hours she could be seen shuffling back and forth in the hall" (p. 236).

Miss Bürstner's status as a typist is mentioned in Kafka's text neutrally (p. 12) and, in the unfinished chapter, with the sexual implication accentuated by Weiss: "K had no desire to exaggerate anything; he knew that Fräulein Bürstner was an ordinary little typist who couldn't resist him for long" (p. 242).

Scene 12

The glimpse of Willem, Franz, and Miss Bürstner in the storeroom alludes overtly to the scene "The Flogger": "K heard the sound of groans behind a door that he had always assumed led to a mere junk room, though he had never seen it himself . . . the scream that Franz expelled rose steady and unchanging, scarcely human, as if it came from some tortured instrument" (pp. 80, 84). The sexualized image in the play may have a source in another unfinished chapter, where K slips into a "half sleep" and sees Miss Bürstner in a group of strangers: "he found her right in the middle of the group, her arms around two men standing on either side of her. That made absolutely no impression on him, particularly because this sight was nothing new, but merely the indelible memory of a photograph on the beach he had once seen in Fräulein Bürstner's room" (p. 262).

Scene 14

Hasterer's evocation of K's family, and the need for K to visit them, echoes a sentence in the novel spoken by K's uncle, who arrives to intervene in the trial: "In any case it would be best for you to take a brief vacation and visit us in the countryside" (p. 93). K's parental background is sketched more fully in the fragmentary chapter on the public prosecutor: "without ever having experienced the care of his own father, who had died quite young, K had left home early, and had always tended to reject rather than elicit the tenderness of his mother, whom he had last visited some two years ago, and who, half blind, still lived out in the small, unchanging village" (p. 250). In the rudimentary chapter "Journey to His Mother," we also learn that "she had become excessively pious" (p. 264).

The closing line of the scene, "Call me Leni," quotes directly, but in a wholly different tone, the seductive nurse of Kafka's lawyer: " 'By the way, call me Leni,' she added abruptly, as if not a moment of their talk should be wasted" (p. 105).

Scene 15

The subterranean "palace" conceived by the miner whose photograph is on K's desk alludes not to *The Trial* but to Kafka's final story, "The Burrow." There the indefatigable builder cannot live in his dream structure but must perpetually guard it against intruders.

Scene 19

While Titorelli is a very different painter from Kafka's character of the same name, one phrase in *The Trial* hints at the creative methods of the figure in the play: "he even told K to make himself comfortable and, when K hesitated, he walked over and pressed him deep into the bedding and pillows" (p. 148).

Scene 33

In the novel, it is K who passes judgment on himself as he is being executed; " 'Like a dog!' he said; it seemed as though the shame was to outlive him" (p. 231).

PETER WEISS ON *THE NEW TRIAL*

When I undertook, eight years ago, to dramatize Kafka's novel *The Trial*, I stayed as close as possible to the original text. I wanted to investigate in what way the book's internal monologue, with its dreamlike reality, could be translated into the concrete texture of stage happenings. I wanted neither to add anything nor to change anything to accord with today's social conditions.

The New Trial follows a completely different path. The only elements I have taken over from the novel are the reference to it in the title, the names of the characters, and—as a core pattern—certain of the dramatic locations. These are deployed as quotations or as a homage to Kafka. The play is dedicated to Franz Kafka.

It is important to note that, apart from these details, the play is completely freestanding: the only significant relationship to Kafka is one of inner affinity. It is a play happening in our own time, in which Josef K and the figures surrounding him are our contemporaries.

The plot sequence, with its stages in the boardinghouse, in the office spaces and assembly halls, recalls events as they were conceived by Kafka; here, however, they occur in a different framework, without mystical or religious overtones.

Invoking such associations, historical sources, spiritual parallels, psychological and musical motifs—that is simply integral to the way I work.

In this play, *The New Trial*, people are portrayed who, under the pressure of the times, are spiritually broken and stumble into violent inner contradictions. Desperately they try to conform to the rules of capitalist society or to break free from its compulsions. All, with the exception of Leni and Titorelli, have become estranged from themselves.

In the figure of Miss Bürstner is portrayed the oppression of women in "patriarchal society." During her professional rise she is forced to deny her status and to play along in the network of mendacity, simply in order to retain her position—until, the moment she is no longer needed, she is expelled anyway.

The hierarchy of the business world is shown as it operates in both the small business and the multinational monopoly, with its mechanism of ruthless upward mobility and obsession with profit, and with the darkness of the human condition coming gradually into the open. The closer we come to the unconcealed language of power, to the absorption of the leading characters into the dynamics of imperialism, the clearer the reference becomes to the monstrous dangers overshadowing our life today.

Josef K becomes increasingly conscious of this process. Initially ensconced in the business world, he is gradually afflicted by doubts. Yet before he recognizes the extent to which he has deceived himself, he also finds himself excluded.

With his ideals, his striving for improvements, his insights into the vast injustices and exploitations occurring everywhere, he has been systematically used by his employers: they have transformed his humanism into their alibi.

A CONVERSATION

between Peter Weiss, Gunilla Palmstierna-Weiss,
and Anita Brundahl (1982)

[Note by Anita Brundahl: Peter Weiss is no surrealist. However, just as the surrealists once did, Gunilla Palmstierna-Weiss and Peter Weiss like to dwell on the beauty of "an unexpected encounter between an umbrella and a sewing machine on an operating table," an encounter that once was staged by Lautréamont. Leading surrealists elevated this phrase to the status of a core principle. In this conversation, we return to the operating table, where sewing machine and umbrella have given way to something else, something unlabeled.]

Anita Brundahl: Ten years of work on the three-volume novel *The Aesthetics of Resistance* and now suddenly: *The New Trial*.

Peter Weiss: It's the most spontaneous and personal play I've ever written. It doesn't have the mass of source materials with which I've normally worked. I wrote *The New Trial* immediately after finishing the proofs of the third volume of *The Aesthetics of Resistance*. *The Aesthetics of Resistance* is a probe into the psyche of specific characters. These are people in the middle of large historical events; however, they're no longer portrayed in an overtly political way, as activists, but as very complicated creatures exposed to the complexities and pressures of the world. Having completed this work, I entered a time of reflection and simultaneously felt a need for something I had really longed for, an urge for purely theatrical form. I have always been powerfully involved with drama as such, even though the form of *The Aesthetics of Resistance*, with its sequence of images and its flow of scenes and events, is surely dramatic in its own way.

Gunilla Palmstierna-Weiss: You've been thinking about the play ever since your old version of *The Trial*.

PW: That's right. But I wanted to render *The Trial* in a completely new way.

The new theme emerged through a conversation with a specialist in economics, but it also has a certain relationship to my work on the novel.

GPW: I'd say you were trying for a synthesis or were returning to an earlier stage of your life—making a connection to the surrealist period. A combination of your older concerns with what you stand for today. You're working again in a particular literary mode, one that you'd set aside many years ago but that became relevant again.

PW: Because something was lacking that is really very important to me.

GPW: That's what I mean. I understand this play as a synthesis of your political self and your older emotional, psychological, and surrealist being. At the time that led you to Goethe, Schiller, Hölderlin, then to the hero of the young, Hermann Hesse; and finally to Franz Kafka, to Henry Miller and others—that period ended with your play *Hölderlin*. For nine years these books stayed in the background, with a quite different literature in the foreground, and now they offer a kind of sounding board again.

AB: You have said yourself on various occasions that Josef K is an ironic self-portrait, as you were but no longer are.

GPW: Even though the characters, because of their names, allude to Kafka's novel—there's much about them that derives from you and your personal view of things, and the play makes many of your unconscious traits visible.

PW: That's also something I haven't wanted to analyze. I know the text is a confrontation with characteristics that I rediscovered in myself; at the same time there's a question that, as a politically committed writer, one often asks oneself: What does one ever actually achieve with one's work? Isn't it condemned to remain esoteric? Bertolt Brecht calls it "tui": the intellectuals have solutions for everything, but when it comes down to it, it's impossible to implement these solutions, they're carried out by others, often by the masses . . .

GPW: If you can even call them solutions.

PW: That's why the chorus is important. There was already the suggestion of a chorus in the first version of *The Trial*. Among others, there was a worker involved. That was the only difference in an otherwise straight stage version of Kafka's novel. In this version the chorus is particularly emphasized.

AB: Aren't there significant contradictions in the things Josef K says?

GPW: There are contradictions in everyone. Not only in Josef K. It's this contradictoriness, these sudden shifts that the actors find hard to manage—and in fact there are contradictions, in every scene. In other words, there are very many levels to which justice must constantly be done.

PW: It is also intrinsic to the play's stylistic principles that the roles display these contradictions. You can see the surrealist principle which is based on confrontations and the collision of contradictions, at work. "The confrontation between a sewing machine and an umbrella on an operating table"—the classic surrealist principle.

GPW: Incidentally: Peter and I first met in the summer of 1952 at a discussion of André Breton and his book Nadja. We decided then that if we ever had a daughter, this would be her name. Nadja was born twenty years later. Surrealism was our first major discussion.

AB: Still, you've both stressed the whole time, very carefully, that the play's style is neither symbolist nor surrealist, while at the same time we as your collaborators have felt a strong need to be given a label defining the basic style.

GPW: Even if one is presumptuous enough to think one is working out a basic style, that still doesn't mean it's "labeled." Indeed, that might be rather difficult.

AB: We noticed that. There's this need to "label" even individual scenes: this is a dream sequence, that's a realistic scene, and so on.

GPW: You can compare the points of contact between Peter's work and mine to a sculpture in the Modern Museum in Stockholm, a construction fusing varied blocks of material that really does represent a unity; and I think you can see this dimension both in the text and in the mise-en-scène—a monumental sculpture standing on the stage, twisting and turning, suffering and living. We could hardly work together if we didn't have a mutual artistic, literary, and social foundation.

So we're not two people who live together, but two independent artists working on a common foundation; but—and here I want to include you, Anita—we could not have realized this project without a practical and organizationally adept discussion partner sharing the same core ideas. That's extraordinarily important.

PW: I share Gunilla's opinion. But I would like to underscore once more how important it is that the play not be labeled surrealist. The fact is, rather, that many people can't see clearly enough to realize how multidimensional and unreal their everyday reality can be.

AB: I think many know this intuitively, but their energies and the situation they're in often don't allow them to express it. The insight seems so absurd that it easily disappears in a washing machine or behind the next street corner. At the point where the boundaries between dream and reality dissolve.

PW: Actually, this play is horribly realistic. Our reality does in fact look like that.

GPW: When I'm sitting in a car and see how the house on the left side is reflected in the windshield, while at the same moment I'm looking at the house on the right side and observing how the passers-by on the street slip through this mirror, this is a straightforward optical perception of reality. That is what reality *is*.

PW: And then there's all that complicated, ambiguous stuff you have inside yourself. This level of perception is one of the basic premises for understanding art, literature, and life in general.

AB: How do we reach all the other collaborators with our discussion of basic styles and formal problems?

GPW: We've established that many people here are working together toward a common goal — people with different backgrounds, different associations, and different assumptions about life. Some of us began with a common denominator. That's exactly what we're searching for. Not for the *lowest* common denominator, but for *a* common denominator. Most of the rehearsal period had passed before we found it.

AB: The larger the ensemble, the more languages there are, if it's even possible to put into words what is happening between the vision and the goal. There are as many ways of working and proceeding as there are people. But ultimately the actor's main method of argument is to provoke and to exemplify a truth on stage, through his work on the role and the commitment of his physical being. Only then does dialogue begin.

PW: The play as such has a stylized form, as does the staging. Or perhaps it should be called a strict style. But its impact must be alive, not mechanical. The style must express the actor's inner self. Only then is it convincing. It took a long time to bring those scenes to life in which we had trouble finding the connection between the role and the actors' own impulses and personal initiatives. We're staging an experiment here, trying to break with all familiar and current dramatic forms. To do something almost impossible.

GPW: We were also all forced to proceed visually in a specific way. We don't have a naturalistic space. The vertical dimension is disproportionate. There's no realism in the lighting or scene changes. Thus there are constant ruptures, when each scene, as you cut away from it, is contrasted with a completely new visual space.

PW: The sculptural model is really predetermined, and it forces the players into a special acting style.

GPW: Another example: the projection screen showing not pictures but, rather, associative images evoking our own time, by which one might be inspired to the creation of pictures. The pictures themselves don't exist, they're only talked about. That makes things hard for the actors. For the public too maybe. Hardest of all perhaps for critics.

AB: The screen was, however, very positively received by the ensemble when it was first installed in the set.

GPW: Our hope was that the actors would feel how monumental the stage set made them. That every movement and gesture would become visible. Being exposed like that can be anxiety provoking, but perhaps inspirational too.

AB: Peter, how do author and director interact?

PW: We've often discussed that. For me the relationship is not at all strange. Because when you write a play, you're also basically directing it as you write. Until now I've only directed films, while assisting with the direction of *The Lusitanian Bogey*; apart from that I preferred to write the plays. As a dramatist I've often attended the production of my plays by other directors. You can imagine how my fingers were itching.

GPW: But directing is also practical work.

PW: Yes, that's a very different aspect.

AB: Wasn't it the case that you contacted the Dramaten, told them about your new play, and said you'd like to try being the director yourself?

PW: Absolutely not. Lasse Pöysti [head of the Dramaten] asked me in the spring of 1981 if I had a new play. It so happened that *The New Trial* had just been finished—I didn't even have copies of it yet. Otherwise nothing would have happened but the nice inquiry. If the play was to be produced, it was clear right away that Gunilla would do the stage set.

GPW: May I perhaps add that direction and stage set engage with each other very strongly. Just as, for Peter, creating the text and imagining the stage set are interwoven processes. We need to find a new form of collaboration between director and designer. It's not just a question of the stage set. For *The New Trial*, for example, we developed the stage set together, through discussion, and that's how we handled the entire production. I have a lot of practical experience in the theater; I've had contact with large technical and managerial systems. Direction isn't just practical and organizational work, doesn't just involve director and performers. This work also makes psychological demands. And without technical knowledge the vision can't be realized.

PW: I was really able to learn a lot of new things!

AB: It was very interesting and rewarding, for example, to read Peter's stage directions in the text before the work of production began.

GPW: A large number of these directions were changed in the course of the practical work.

PW: Our work was an ongoing discussion among all involved. You can call it collaboration, an experiment in democracy. We tell each other our ideas, we criticize each other. We enrich each other. In the end we're all responsible for the project.

GPW: But that means each individual must take responsibility for his or her special task. We have a basic discussion on which we build. Direction, stage design, and acting style are completely integrated with each other. But everything we see on stage is ultimately subordinate to the word, to the word's meaning, the word's rhythm. Without that there'd be no theater, at least no spoken theater.

AB: Peter, how did you proceed with the sound mixing? At an early stage, in April 1981, we talked of having a special composition produced. I'd suggested the names of some composers, but you had reservations. In the end you did it yourself, working with the sound technician and the studio manager Ulla Cederlund. We're all impressed by your musical knowledge.

PW: I'm glad that we produced almost the entire soundtrack before beginning rehearsals. Many people drape the sound over a production at the end, like a kind of decoration.

AB: Or they use sound effects or music as an accompaniment. Here sound was integral to the whole.

PW: I did it this way also with the experimental films I made in the late 1950s. Gunilla was involved in them too.

AB: What did you gain from working on *The New Trial*, and where may it lead?

PW: For me it's been a great experience, and I regret only that I couldn't have done it ten or twenty years earlier. I certainly could have learned a lot for my craft as a dramatist. I'm really not a director in the conventional sense. I'm anti-authoritarian.

AB: Direction is also the art of listening.

GPW: To me this proves the importance of an experienced ensemble, used to working together, an interaction of people with similar aesthetic, political, or ideological points of view. Just think of Brecht's collaboration with the Berliner Ensemble. It was no accident that this brief time, during which he had his own ensemble with a background identical to his own, was the peak of his dramatic work. As long as we have a repertory theater in its current form, we must try to generate group energies that can coalesce around various specific projects.

AB: Do you mean the type of repertory theater that the Dramaten represents, or are you endorsing the criticism of large institutional theaters?

GPW: No, not at all. I have absolutely nothing against the institutional theater, with its valuable professional expertise and technical skills all concentrated under one roof. We need to defend that. But what we also need is a new type of repertory theater. The current habit of immediately tearing apart groups of people just as soon as they have in some way achieved a common purpose—that's what we must reject.

PW: The conception of an Artists' Theater is absolutely right. That doesn't mean every theater has to be structured like that. But I believe there are many people interested in working in this new way.

AB: So where are the obstacles?
GPW: It is above all a question of organization.
PW, GPW, AB: And it needs continuous work.

Translation of Jörg Scherzer's German text
based on the Swedish original

PETER WEISS ON DRAMATIC STYLE

The stage as such is already an abstraction. A naturalistic play: in the guidance of the dialogue, in the emphatic voicing of the characters, in the movements and gestures—in all that dwells an anachronism.

"Natural" theater has always powerfully modified reality: the theater of antiquity, the theater of African, Asian, and Latin American peoples.

A heightening of reality: the creation of an *autonomous space* with its own laws, with "altered" voices, with intensifying gestures and an autonomous verbal rhythm; playing in the naturalistic style, with a mass of recognizable details, with voices that belong to our everyday experience—all this can be adequate for certain texts.

I speak here of traditional theater, of theater of illusion, of imitation of the everyday, of transposing everyday events into a "museum" in order to present them photographically.

As soon as the stage picture contains strong abstract elements—so that the action, character relationships, and dialogue have a validity other than the one familiarly surrounding us—we have to find a style appropriate to the framework.

    Much of what is said is "quoted"
    or "raised to a different level"
    or "recited"
    or "spoken in the rhythms of a choral work."

From time to time, as interruptions, there can be short sections with brief exchanges that have an almost "everyday" effect—but immediately achieve a quite different "unfamiliar, non-everyday" linguistic profile.

    Movements underline words
    words are made vivid by means of movements

Hence: "an action is to be demonstrated." It is to be portrayed not through empathy but primarily through *technique*. With control: control of gestures, techniques of speech.

The text must first be read: as scientific reports, to be investigated, analyzed.

Against "feeling." Strong emotions must be *enacted*, not experienced. The violent changes within the characters are not to be shown psychologically but must be demonstrated technically!

For example: Miss Montag's great speech in scene 24: do it demagogically rather than expressively. It must of course grab the audience. But not through numbing the mind. The effect is to be one of intellectual brilliance.

In summary: the goal is a realistic but not a naturalistic theater.

Translation of Jörg Scherzer's German text
based on the Swedish original

PETER WEISS ON SOME ROLES
IN *THE NEW TRIAL*
Sketches by Gunilla Palmstierna-Weiss

Josef K

Why is Josef K supported in the firm? Why is he permitted to rise in the
hierarchy and given a directorial position? He really does not provide
much evidence of business accomplishments!

The public prosecutor, who has known K for a long time, understands
his qualities best. He sees how they can be deployed to the firm's advantage. Ultimately, the fact is that such firms want to appear in a
positive, conciliatory light. They adorn themselves with slogans like
humane, progressive, peace loving, and the like. Thus the public
prosecutor (as the opaque highest boss) can use definitions, expert
opinions, reflections, and so on provided by K for the firm's propaganda. K writes good monthly reports, has a mass of idealistic
thoughts that can be used to give the firm a vaguely positive face.

K, as the eternal idealist, is exploited by the firm without really knowing
this himself. He feels doubt and reluctance but nevertheless believes
he is doing good, helping people, working toward something better.
The public prosecutor is at the top of the power structure; under him
is the director, then Rabensteiner. They all convey to K the impression
that he is important and welcome, but really K ought to see through
the performance at an early stage. This he does not do. It is Leni who
clarifies for him what is going on.

When he begins to realize in what way he is being absorbed into the multinational group of companies, it is already too late. Ambitious as he is,
he gives his all, whereupon he is liquidated—when he reveals that he
has seen through the whole thing. Even his murder occurs, as it were,
incidentally. No judge or murderer is seen. K is hit by a stray bullet,
and this too occurs without a specific sign or warning. One hears a

Josef K

few shots and he lies down. Nothing dramatic. He simply lies down as if to sleep—in the fetal position. He is neither hero nor victim; he is a marginal figure, exploited for others' purposes and discarded when he is no longer needed. He is *not a tragic figure.*

K has to find a *basic attitude*, one that he assumes now and again, as if he wanted to collect himself, one that becomes recognizable; its model: a ballet dancer just before a significant movement.

Miss Bürstner

She is the *exploited woman.* She is given authority—but only apparently so.

She remains in a condition of dependence on men. Miss Bürstner tries to free herself but is compelled constantly to adapt. Hence her disturbed character. The rapid alternations between repression and revolt.

Her development shows how she grows—rises higher—but only as long as she serves the male power structure (the hierarchy).

When she has been sufficiently exploited—in the process however, achieving simultaneously the highest possible position in the hierarchy—she is overthrown. Discarded by the men like a used-up commodity.

Miss Bürstner

Rabensteiner

Rabensteiner

It is not completely clear what position Rabensteiner holds. Only at the end does it become obvious that he belongs to the power elite.

He always appears a few levels above K—as his colleague, yet with a slight undertone of dominance. He is friendly, conciliatory, smiles ingratiatingly—and now and again, for a few seconds, his superior position becomes drastically evident. Brief threats, for example. His position is only hinted at in a gesture or turn of phrase. Or in often barely noticeable movements of the action—for example, when, after K's story about the underground palace, Rabensteiner suddenly stands behind him. It is clearer when he throws some papers out of K's desk drawer and K dives after them.

Rabensteiner's task is to transmit the impression that K will belong to the community of the ruling elite. K must be propelled upward as far as possible. He is to contribute as much as possible of his special capabilities, namely, to formulate slogans and images of goodness, optimism, and humane values. His ideas are deployed—that is, distorted—by the propaganda apparatus.

K's insecurity really derives from the questions he puts to himself: What do they really want from me? What can I give? Why am I so well thought of? He has more and more doubts. And when doubt becomes dominant, his power is simply disconnected. For a while even his doubts are usable. For he is so human, so "moving." Think of the statements emanating from American ruling circles or from South African officials: always obliging, courteous, understanding. Through K's statements the concept of "critique" is kept alive. Critique is so good, so important. By resisting the fade-out of critique, we show how democratic we are.

Regime of Lies
Everything is the regime of lies. K is completely enclosed in the web of lies.

Franz and Willem
They represent muscularity, strength, and violence; they constitute a fixed pair. They speak to each other and not to those who address them. They toss their rejoinders to each other. Their movements are uniform.

The pair represent the nucleus of paramilitary organization, that is, of fascism.

Franz and Willem

The Family

The Family

The husband, the wife, the two old people, and the two children constitute the core of society and represent the center of the political
   meetings.

The family stands for all those who constantly have the wool pulled over
   their eyes by the parties.

They must absorb some of the comments that are distributed among the
   anonymous chorus.

When the family, that is, the segment of society subjugated by the ruler,
   is driven out of Josef K's room, they are humiliated.

Through its strong resistance, which is broken at the rulers' orders, the
   family illustrates how injustice and violence come down on human
   beings again and again, drive them to flight or to ruin.

REFLECTIONS ON
A DIRECTOR'S PROCESS
Jody McAuliffe

In 1996, a member of the German department at Duke University approached me about directing a play by Peter Weiss as the centerpiece of a conference on Weiss and his work to be held in the fall of 1998. *The New Trial* stood out from the list of his works. As I do not know German, I asked one of the graduate students on the committee putting the conference together to read it and give me a synopsis. Her report about a modern-day Josef K unwittingly moving up the ladder of an increasingly globalized corporation, a humanist searching for purpose and meaning in the workplace in a world where the distinction between work and life has become blurred, a would-be artist caught in the grip of a multinational, capitalistic corporation in the throes of global expansion, struck a deep chord in me. It sounded so far ahead of its time, this trial with no judges, so immediate to our present global village. Weiss, in his self-avowed most spontaneous and personal piece, had proven, through his distrust of the parties in the play, eerily prescient of the collapse of the Soviet Union and the tearing down of the Berlin Wall. He had seen the future clearly: the pollenization of the world with rampant capitalism, American style, and the consequent destruction of Josef K, the eternal idealist who fails to see through the performances of those who exploit him, the man who carried out with precision the duties he did not understand. This was the play I decided to direct.

This is indeed a strange way to choose a script—without reading it—but since it had yet to be translated, I had to rely on my strong intuition about the play, my fascination with its autobiographical nature, my love of Kafka's novel, and the cultural and historical significance of the fact that it was Weiss's last play and had never been seen in the

United States—a country where it needed to be seen. It was proposed to James Rolleston that he translate the work, and he agreed. All my expectations were fulfilled when I read the draft, though I did find the ending puzzling.

We asked Gunilla Palmstierna-Weiss if she would consider recreating her original design for the production in Sheafer Theater at Duke. For various reasons (among others, that Gunilla's design was for a huge proscenium stage and our theater was a black box), this did not work out. We hired a gifted young designer, a recent graduate of the Yale School of Drama, to design both sets and costumes. Nevertheless, Gunilla was an invaluable resource for me in this production process. When she came to Duke, the most startling and richly important feeling I had after meeting with her was that I felt as if I had met with Peter Weiss himself, so completely did she convey his presence and consciousness to me, as though she carried his spirit within her. We spoke with each other in Sheafer Theater, and she shared with me photographs and slides from the original production and books of Weiss's paintings as a way of beginning our conversation about the play and the history of its production. She told me the story of how Ingmar Bergman talked about the casting of the character of Leni, that you had to know the actress was capable of the scream (the final moment of the play), and then the rest of the development of the character would unwind backward from that to her first appearance. I did not know what she was talking about but thankfully overcame my embarrassment to ask what scream she referred to. I confessed I did not recall any scream. Gunilla told me that in the final stage directions, Leni hurries in after K is shot. "She kneels down beside him. Touches his face. Suddenly stiffens. Then she thrusts her clenched fists into the air. Utters a terrible cry. Darkness." As it turned out, Suhrkamp Verlag had published a version of the text without the last page (without the shooting of K and Leni's scream). No wonder I had found the ending puzzling. Suhrkamp had never recalled the texts with the mistake. The missing page with the crucial information put us in an utterly Kafkaesque situation, from which Gunilla rescued us. It was she who gave us the ending, who gave us the scream of rebellion, that consummate theatrical gesture at the end of this play that the actress Judy Hu realized with such chilling finality. Without that conversation, we would have missed the whole point of the play: that Leni survives and screams out against this anonymous shooting of K in the chaotic crossfire of the fascistic turn of the corporation's expansion. Two fists in the air above her head over the lifeless body of K, she will not be silenced. She has the last sound.

On 3 July 1981, Peter Weiss and Gunilla Palmstierna-Weiss wrote to Stellan Skarsgaard, the actor cast as K, prior to rehearsals for the original production. This letter became the basis for my own work in creating the style of the play.

"The whole planning of the piece will start with the visual." (PW/GPW).

When I met with the designer, Walt Spangler, in Sheafer Theater, first he, and then I, got very excited about the possibilities of the space: the industrial look of the catwalk and the upper deck (what was usually the offstage area for technicians in this black box space). What if that became the corporation, the architecture of the room the site of that mechanized and controlling activity? One of the thrilling conceits of Orson Welles's 1963 film of *The Trial* was that all locations seemed to be absurdly connected. It all took place in one place: this was our solution to the problem of how to achieve the world of this multiple-location play architecturally in one black box space with little capacity for flying scenery in and out of the playing area, while guaranteeing a swift movement from scene to scene and location to location.

For this play, I collaborated with the set designer more than I ever had before with specific regard to how scenes would be staged. In this we followed directly in the footsteps of Peter Weiss and Gunilla Palmstierna-Weiss as a directing team, understanding that design was inextricable from directing, that the designer too had in some sense to direct. Walt did a series of sketches of how each scene would work in the design, with a description of the quality and direction of light for each scene. In scene 4, the desk flies in, descending in front of K as he runs on a treadmill to his office. In scene 6, the desk hangs surrealistically, like a guillotine over K's existence. In scene 9, the characters in the boardinghouse move all the way around the island of K's room. There is no privacy here; he is completely exposed. In scene 10, the warehouse takes over his room: K watching his late-night show on a portable television in his room transitions to the assembly room with the company piling in, bringing the meeting with them, the blue flicker from the television growing to become the flicker of unseen overhead fans with light passing through them, the ensemble perching on top of K's furniture. At the end of act 1, when Rabensteiner is cleaning out K's desk, the desk is literally floating off the floor; we are caught between the world of the boardinghouse and that of the office. Rabensteiner has to stand on something to rifle the desk properly. By act 2, the boundary between K's office and his room has been so thoroughly eroded that Leni inhabits his room, his bed, as if it were part of the office. The boundaries of his room, like the boundaries of his personality, are completely fluid. In scene 17, K and Leni are at first in his office having sex as they discuss parties and art. Eventually people emerge—surrounding them—until they are in the meeting room once again. Walt first described this controversial staging, not specified by Weiss, in his sketch describing the transition between scenes 16, K's office, and 17, the warehouse. Details from the sex scene between K and Leni in Kafka's novel provided stage directions for me, and this behavior greased the transition between the two locations, which, as Leni indicates, are actually connected: the corporation controls the party. A sharp tension, a subtle antagonism, was generated between what K and Leni were saying and what they were doing. Leni describes how the party lodges the bait in the throats of unsuspecting fish, hooks them in their mouths, and pulls them upward into the open air of a meeting, just as she leads K to a passionate kiss from which they break apart, K gasping for air. Though Leni is with K at the public prosecutor's behest—in order to hook K into casting off his tendency to become distracted from the corporate task at hand (a plan that, of course, backfires)—she is his only hope for salvation, for a deep breath of fresh air.

When the family comes to live with K, they move all the furniture off the room platform as the desk looms. When Miss Montag speaks, she stands in a cold spotlight in the center aisle among the audience; we are all participants in the party meetings. When I mentioned to Gunilla the connection I saw between Kurt Joos's ballet *The Green Table* and the conference table scenes, she concurred that the analogy was there. My memory of the choreography inspired the staging in scene 26. The image I had for scene 31 was always that of the corporate bigwigs out on the golf course deciding the fate of the world.

Gunilla and I talked about the complex design problem presented by the presence of Titorelli's paintings, that whenever we actually have to see the work of the artist in a play we run the risk of disappointing the audience. Gunilla solved this problem by using a collage of paintings and politically charged photographs. Walt and I decided to have the paintings be clear vinyl stretched over wooden frames. When the company brought the paintings on stage, they assumed various poses for a few moments, some as described in the play (the bank employee, Miss Bürstner, and the cripple, Miss Montag, pressed into the colors . . . you see "stomach, sex, thighs"), while leaving invisible traces of their hands and pressing each other up against the vinyl canvases. The entire ensemble participated with their whole bodies in the depravity of art. The paintings were alive and also blank—so much easier for the corporation to coopt through ownership.

What Titorelli paints is also what the Woman cleans up in the toilet: filth and vomit. For Titorelli, art is a substitute for life; it is depravity. K wants to see purity and clarity in art but is afraid of participating in it. His lifelong search is for meaning. Titorelli, by contrast, is completely empty. He has renounced all meaning and embraced sensuality. In the final analysis, it is Leni who achieves the synthesis of these two positions. She urges K to accept everything, reject nothing. K, forever searching for a third possibility with Miss Bürstner, emotionally and sexually, gets caught in the crossfire, unable to make a move. When K actually touches the paint on one of Titorelli's paintings, he is terrified.

"That that which is said, that that which exists in inner tensions is expressed in very clear—sometimes overemphasized and 'overdriven' movements is very important" (PW/GPW).

One of the greatest obstacles I faced in mounting this production was that I was dealing with an undergraduate cast, some with no stage experience, and most with no understanding of a play of this kind—a highly political and highly expressionistic work. My students, by and large, had never even heard of Brecht, let alone Weiss. To rock them out of their 1998 American realism was a formidable task. In 1980, I had directed Brecht's *Drums in the Night*, a decidedly more poetic text than *The New Trial*. Though both plays demand an intensely physical, highly choreographed style, my approach to *The New Trial*, with its emphasis on overdriven, overemphasized movements, had to be different. Weiss described his distinguishing demand on the actors and director: "Since the figures are composed of antagonisms, these must necessarily stand out with sudden changes in the treatment of language as well as in body language."

To develop a "homogeneous style, a homogeneous language" for this "very concrete piece, very physical, very 'gestured,'" like that described to Skarsgaard by Peter Weiss and Gunilla Palmstierna-Weiss, I posed a series of questions and exercises to the actors. I asked them to fill in the blanks to a series of questions and to make lists: "When I think of Kafka, I see ——, I hear ——, I smell ——." Other subject areas were political parties, corporations, family, and for K, Dante's *Inferno*—the structural model for the play. I also asked them to develop a series of gestures for each subject. I asked them to see *Brazil*, *The Trial*, *Kafka*, *Marat/Sade*, *The Truman Show*, and *Dr. Strangelove*, to build common bodies of imagery from which I could draw. I asked the entire cast to read something by Kafka and distributed to them Weiss's notes on Josef K, Miss Bürstner, Rabensteiner, the Regime of Lies, Franz and Willem, and the family.

In rehearsal I worked a series of improvisations based on these topics, using the language and gestures the students had prepared, accompanied by the music of Spring Heel Jack and Erik Satie, between which I abruptly alternated. Slowly, a common language developed. This way of being, this behavior, translated directly into the staging. At one point, the actor playing the captain had a major breakthrough in scene 2 when he realized I actually wanted him to execute specific gestures he had developed through these exercises in the scene. They were, of course, not illustrative, but revelatory and intriguing, and, according to the physical logic of the world we were creating in response to the play, totally correct.

The body silhouettes for the characters were created in response to the word and embodied their moral stance. Weiss said, "That which is said stands and moves in a room." He thought of "the word's bodily language," and we created the look for each character. Walt and I agreed that Josef K's basic look should be from the period of the novel, and that the silhouettes of the other characters should reach forward from that time into the contemporary scene. K looked as Rabensteiner described him: like a man who did not live in the same time as the rest of them.

Just as Stellan Skarsgaard, the original K, was the linchpin for the original production, Eamonn Farrell was that for mine. Eamonn, a dancer as well as an actor and director, grasped the "basic attitude" called for by Weiss: "one that he assumes now and again, as if he wanted to collect himself, one that becomes recognizable; its model: a ballet dancer just before a significant movement." This active interiority juxtaposed against the physical tension of preparation is the very condition that allows K to miss the fact that Kaminer, to whom K has entrusted the family, pushes the group out roughly, with no intention of taking them to the cashier. Eamonn, who is reminiscent of Buster Keaton, especially when he falls out of bed while eavesdropping on Miss Bürstner and the captain mauling each other offstage in scene 7, had that open gaze the director sees in K. The poster for the production surrealistically captured Eamonn's stunned face larger than life, held captive inside a skyscraper.

Another important revelation from Welles's film interpretation was K's overpowering erotic need for, and his involvement with, oversexed women. That translated into the look of Miss Bürstner, Weiss's tragic heroine—in silk robe, 1960s go-go girl look, and corporate chic. Her sexuality is the key to her success and her downfall. Miss Montag—in a sheer, clingy dress and a leg brace—looks like somebody out of David Cronenberg's *Crash*, embodying the tension between disfigurement and desire.

The look of the corporation figures was inspired by Georg Grosz's paintings. The director had an exaggerated high, stiff collar and lipstick. Rabensteiner had a sunburnt face, lined lips, cinched waist, and painted fingernails. Adam Saunders, who played Rabensteiner, developed a frightening pattern of sudden, unexpected gestures that constituted brief threats. Just as Rabensteiner's role in the hierarchy is hidden at first, his true nature only comes out in these gestures, which in their suddenness and overdrivenness communicated the antagonisms, the hostile forces at work against K and the family. In the scene at the top of act 2, Rabensteiner tortures K as if they were in the "Penal Colony," with Rabensteiner grinding his feet into the floor while K experiences his movement in the same way the prisoner in Kafka's story experiences the lacerating writing on his back.

Wearing a Warholesque wig and an expensive white suit, the public prosecutor lapses into a few sudden Hitlerian gestures as he tries to persuade K to his nonviolent spiritual colonization, his final solution. Kaminer, the buttinsky, sported an extended nose. Franz and Willem, perverse twins in orange jumpsuits, then orange business suits, who seem by turns comic and then threatening, speak primarily to each other, not to those who address them. We decided the family should be nouveau poor, one that had had money and then lost it suddenly and irrevocably. This notion felt appropriately contemporary. The heavy padding of the members of the boardinghouse, the captain and Mrs. Grubach, heightened their unreality. The party speaker was a black woman in paramilitary garb. We made the ambassador a woman to add more variety to the corporate panel as well as distinguish her as specifically American, a suggestion of Madeleine Albright. Finally, after much consideration, at Walt's suggestion we made the general a puppet: this gave him the surreal quality of the geometric characters in Grosz's paintings and guaranteed that his entrance would have the impact suggested by the script. The irony of having the ultimate one in control not be in control of himself was deeply resonant. Steve Heasley, the actor playing the captain, did a brilliant job of manipulating the puppet—a truly frightening and unsettling image.

"Short sound effects will connect/guide the different scenes. Stark contrasts, changes, antitheses even here" (PW/GPW).

Starting with the mysterious humming K alone hears, the sound design for The New Trial presented some interesting problems. The sounds, like the figures, are composed of antagonisms: Miss Bürstner's laughter turns to crying; the family's monotonous, rhythmic groaning turns into something like a chorus or a liturgy; the whispering, heavy breathing, and panting in scene 7 could also be a scraping and scratching of objects being pushed around. The aural aspect of this world is strange and mysterious. The actors made these sounds live.

Gunilla said that Peter Weiss had developed a sound score for the transitions out of those human sounds. After much deliberation, I decided on the more formal, less human choice of the antagonism between the highly mechanized, driving, contemporary music of Spring Heel Jack (the corporation) and the lyrically simple *Gymnopédies* of Erik Satie (Titorelli's studio, scenes with Leni), plus a little Diamanda Galás for subjective, strangely operatic angst.

One of the many successes of the production was that the students acted with their bodies, something that impressed Gunilla very much. The students had contacted the reality of Weiss's world and incarnated his consciousness in their work. *The New Trial* is art about art. At the heart of K's struggle is whether or not art can have any impact on political life. This work, like Racine's plays, restores the moral role of theater in the community. Some audience members commented on how much the corporation and its lack of humanity reminded them of managed health care.

Leni carries within her Weiss's final vision of his life as an artist: that art fills the being of the artist, lightens the burden for the moment, and gives the possibility that it might endure. This play is the swan song of a life in which Weiss gave himself to art. How achingly powerful that it ends with a scream. When the cast presented me with a silver photo album as a memento, the quote that summed up the experience for all of us was engraved on the cover: "You should give yourself completely to your terrible love, even if it destroys you." This production was a testament to Weiss's enduring gift to us all.

Peter Weiss was a German playwright, dramatist, and novelist who died in 1982. He wrote a number of works in German, many of which have been translated into English. They include *The Leavetaking* (1962); *Vanishing Point* (1962); *The Persecution and Assassination of Jean-Paul Marat . . . (Marat/Sade)* (1965); *The Investigation* (1966); *Trotsky in Exile* (1968); *Limited Bombing in Vietnam* (1969); *Notes on the Cultural Life of the Democratic Republic of Vietnam* (1970); *Song of the Lusitanian Bogey* and *Discourse of the Prolonged War of Liberation in Viet Nam . . .* (published in one volume, 1970); *The Conversation of the Three Walkers* and *The Shadow of the Coachman's Body* (published in one volume as *Bodies and Shadows* [1970]); *American Presence in South East Asia* (1971); and *Ästhetik des Widerstands* (1975–81).

James Rolleston is Professor and Chair of German at Duke University. He has written books on Kafka, on the young Rilke, and on modern German poetry. His previous book-length translation, of *Walter Benjamin: An Intellectual Biography*, by Bernd Witte (Wayne State UP, 1991) won the German Literary Prize of the American Translators Association in 1993.

Kai Evers is a graduate student in the Department of Germanic Languages and Literatures at Duke University.

Library of Congress Cataloging-in-Publication Data
Weiss, Peter, 1916–82
[Neue Prozess. English]
The new trial / Peter Weiss ; translated, with an introduction, by James Rolleston and Kai Evers.
ISBN 0-8223-2681-7 (alk. paper) —
ISBN 0-8223-2690-6 (pbk. : alk. paper)
I. Rolleston, James, 1939–   II. Evers, Kai.   III. Title.
PT2685.E5 W49913 2001   832'.914—dc21   00-045187